Rodel Rodis

Book 1

22-Articles
Random Dates

Rodel Rodis

Published by

TATAY JOBO ELIZES.
*Self-Publisher
in 2017, under the
permission and authorization*
of RODEL RODIS,
author and owner of the copyright to this book. The copyright owner can withdraw this permission at his discretion without any objection from Talay Jobo Elizes at any time. Printing of this book is using the present day method of Print-On-Demand (POD) system, where prints will never run out of copies to be available for posterity. The copyright owner is free to republish with other publishers anytime.

*ISBN - 13: 978 - 1976564369
ISBN - 10: 1976564360*

*Contact: job_elizes@yahoo.com
Website: http://tinyurl.com/mj76ccq*

Special Note

Articles are arranged at random dates

Contents

ooooo

About the Author

Rodel Rodis is a lawyer and writer with his own blogsite. He is active member in several egroups.

He served as Board president for three terms and was chair of the California Community College Trustees Association.

He taught Philippine History at San Francisco State University.

Rodel Rodis is the President of the Global Filipino Diaspora Council (GFDC) & organizes Filipino Diaspora conferences and Diaspora councils in all the continents from Europe to the Middle East, Asia, Oceania, Africa and North America.

ooooo

Send comments to Rodel50@gmail.com or mail them to the Law Offices of Rodel Rodis at 2429 Ocean Avenue, San Francisco, CA 94127 or call 415.334.7800.

Most my articles are published at:
www.globalnation.inquirer.net,
usp4gg@yahoogroups.com,
globalfildiaspora@yahoogroups.com,
ateneoforbetterphilippines@yahoogroups.com,
FilipinoAmerican_Network@yahoogroups.com,
all@naffaa.org

1
Why China Will Declare War If PH Drills for Oil
June 7, 2017

On May 19, 2017, President Rodrigo Duterte disclosed at a press conference in Manila that he met with Chinese President Xi Jinping during the "One Belt, One Road" summit in Beijing on May 15 and told Xi of his country's intention to drill for oil in the West Philippine Sea.

"We intend to drill oil there, if it's yours, well, that's your view, but my view is, I can drill the oil, if there is some inside the bowels of the earth, because it is ours," Duterte said he told Xi.

"His response to me, 'we're friends, we don't want to quarrel with you, we want to maintain the presence of warm relationship, but if you force the issue, we'll go to war," Duterte said.

https://www.youtube.com/watch?v=DSG

Xi's threat was unmistakable. This was Xi's message: "We're friends as long as you accept the fact that the South China Sea is ours, all of it including the portion you call the West Philippine Sea. As long as you accept this, we will provide you with generous loans to fund your infrastructure projects. But if you drill for oil there, we will declare war on you."

Why did Duterte disclose Xi's threat when he had been extolling the leadership of Xi and had been moving the Philippines away from the United States towards his embrace of China?

Why did Xi risk alienating his closest ally in Southeast Asia by openly threatening him with war if he asserted sovereignty over his country's territorial waters?

Xi may recall that when Duterte visited China on a state visit in October 2016, he announced his military and economic "separation" from the U.S. "America has lost now. I've realigned myself in your ideological flow. And maybe I will also go to Russia to talk to Putin and tell him that there are three of us against the world: China, Philippines and Russia. It's the only way."

Just three weeks earlier, on April 29, 2017, at the opening of the Summit of the Association of Southeast Asian Nations (ASEAN) in Manila, Duterte told reporters that the there was "no point" for ASEAN to protest Chinese artificial island building in disputed areas of the South China Sea because ASEAN was "helpless" to stop China.

"It cannot be an issue anymore. It's already there. What would be the purpose also of discussing it if you cannot do anything," Duterte said referring to China's transformation of reefs and shoals in areas of the sea claimed by the Philippines and other nations into artificial islands, and installing military facilities there.

The United States and other nations have criticized China's militarization of the waterway where $5 trillion in annual trade passes as a serious threat to freedom of navigation. China's Foreign Ministry spokeswoman Hua Chunying did not dispute the essence of the Xi-Duterte conversation but described it merely as part of their agreement to "strengthen communication" on important bilateral issues.

Duterte's new Secretary of Foreign Affairs former Sen. Alan Peter Cayetano echoed the Chinese version saying "The conversation was very frank. There was mutual respect, there was mutual trust," Cayetano told reporters even though he was not present when the conversation occurred.

"The context was not threatening each other, that we will go to war. The context is how do we stabilize the region and how do we prevent conflict," Cayetano added.

What the Chinese and Philippine foreign ministries will not answer is the question WHY.

The answer can be found in a news article that appeared on May 18, 2017 entitled "China successfully mines flammable ice from the South Sea"

http://www.mining.com/china-success...

"In a first for the country, engineers extracted the gas from the so-called "flammable ice" – methane hydrate, where the gas is trapped in ice crystals – and converted it to natural gas in a single, continuous operation on a floating production platform.

After nearly two decades of research and exploration, China has successfully mined so-called "flammable ice" in what authorities qualify as a major breakthrough that may lead to a global energy revolution.

The element, a kind of natural gas hydrate, was discovered in the area in 2007, but this is the first time the country is able to successfully extract combustible ice from the seabed, in a single, continuous operation on a floating production platform in the Shenhu area of the South China Sea, about 300km southeast of Hong Kong, state-run Xinhua news agency reports."

Methane hydrate global sources are estimated to exceed the combined energy content of all other fossil fuels."

Estimates of the South China Sea's methane hydrate potential now range as high as 150 billion cubic meters of natural gas equivalent, sufficient to satisfy China's entire equivalent oil consumption for 50 years.

The commercial production of methane hydrate would reduce China's dependence on energy imports, which accounts for nearly 60% of its crude oil needs, making it the world's No. 2 importer by volume, after the U.S.

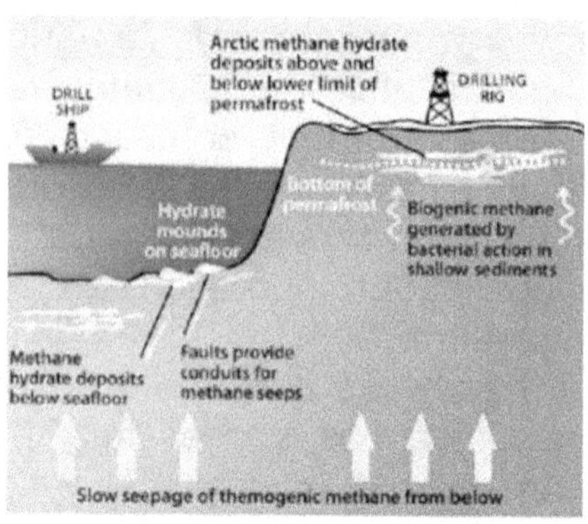

Methane hydrate will also aid China's efforts to shift to natural gas from coal, which accounts for nearly 70% of its primary-energy consumption, which has caused harmful pollution to China's cities.

China's discovery of methane hydrates off the coasts of Vietnam and the Philippines is what has prompted China to aggressively pursue the occupation of Philippine and Vietnamese shoals and their conversion to artificial islands in order to safely conduct its exploration and production of methane hydrate.

This explains China's placement of an oil rig platform off the coast of Vietnam which triggered international showdowns with Vietnam.

The Recto Bank (Reed Bank) area located only 50 miles west of the Philippine island of Palawan is considered a methane hydrate honey pot. The Philippines estimates that the Sampaguita Field within Recto Bank may also hold large deposits of natural gas equivalents in the form of methane hydrates.

The oil found in the Malampaya oil field off the Palawan coast already accounts for 40% of the energy needs of Luzon. The methane hydrates in Recto Bank will make the Philippines not only energy self-sufficient but can generate revenue from its export.

This is why Pres. Benigno Aquino Jr. warned China in his State of the Nation Address (SONA) in July 2011 that "if you set foot in Recto Bank, it will be as if you set foot on Recto Avenue. What's ours is ours."

Philippine Supreme Court Justice Antonio Carpio urged the Philippine government on May 20 to sue China for threatening war against the Philippines over the West Philippine Sea dispute.

Carpio wrote, "As a nation that under its Constitution has renounced war as an instrument of national policy, the Philippines' recourse is to bring China's threat of war to another UNCLOS arbitral tribunal, to secure an order directing China to comply with the ruling of the UNCLOS arbitral tribunal that declared the Reed Bank part of Philippine EEZ."

The UNCLOS tribunal at the Permanent Court of Arbitration in The Hague, Netherlands, ruled unanimously in July 2016 that China's expansive claim over the entire South China Sea was invalid but China has rejected the UN ruling.

Justice Carpio also urged the Philippine government to bring China's threat to go to war before the United Nations General Assembly by "sponsoring a resolution condemning China's threat of war against the Philippines and demanding that China comply with the ruling of the UNCLOS arbitral tribunal."

Filipinos in New York plan to rally in front of the United Nations on June 12 at noon to denounce China's threat of war against the Philippines.

"We are holding our rally fittingly on June 12 Philippine Independence Day because we want to show the world that while Filipinos fought for our independence from Spain in 1898, we will also fight for our independence from China in 2017," declared Loida Nicolas Lewis, national chair of the US Pinoys for Good Governance (USP4GG).

Independence Day protest rallies have been scheduled in front of the Philippine Embassy in Washington DC and in Philippine Consulates throughout the US simultaneously at noon on June 12.

If the Philippines does not protest China's threat of war, it will mean that the Philippines is surrendering its sovereignty to China. ."Acquiescence means the Philippines will lose forever its EEZ in the West Philippine Sea to China," Justice Carpio said.

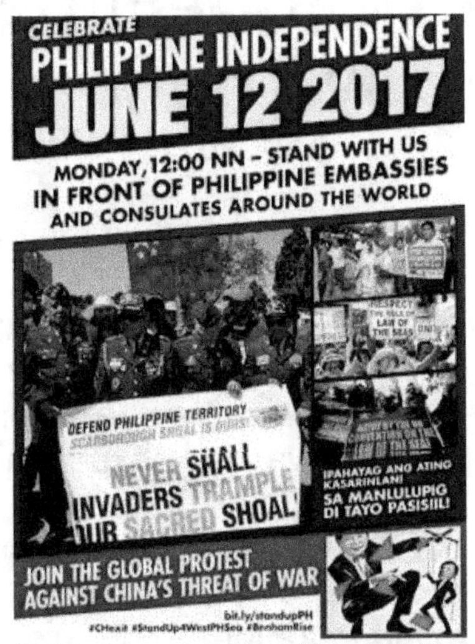

(Celebrate June 12 Philippine Independence Day by asserting Philippine Independence from China. Join the global protest rallies in front of your local Philippine consulates. Log on to USPGG.org for more information. Send comments to Rodel50@gmail.com or mail them to the Law Offices of Rodel Rodis at 2429 Ocean Avenue, San Francisco, CA 94127 or call 415.334.7800)

Ooooo

2
TNTs Fear Deportation by Trump
Feb. 2017

The Filipino colloquial term for a deportable alien in the U.S. is "TNT", short for "*Tago ng Tago*" or always hiding. It also stands for "*Takot na Takot*" or very afraid. Both translations vividly describe the traumatic fear deportable aliens have been experiencing since President Trump's Immigration and Customs Enforcement (ICE) agents began rounding up TNTs from countries all over the world one week after Trump's inauguration.

The February 13, 2017 New York Times headline "Undocumented Immigrants Rounded Up" would not technically describe Filipino TNTs because, unlike their Mexican counterparts who crossed over the land border from their homeland by foot, Filipinos entered through airports with passport documents, the status explained in Filipino filmmaker Jose Antonio Vargas' CNN documentary "Documented".

But the inaccurate term is still preferable to "illegal aliens" because, as Nobel Peace Prize winner and Holocaust survivor Elie Wiesel said, "no human being is illegal". Also, in a 2012 immigration decision of the U.S. Supreme Court, Justice Anthony M. Kennedy noted in the majority opinion, "As a general rule, it is not a crime for a removable alien to remain present in the United States." It is a civil offense, not a criminal one.

Despite the US Supreme Court ruling, Trump still insists that he is cracking down on "illegal criminals".

In his January 25, 2017 Executive Order about building the Mexico border wall, Trump included a provision vastly expanding the definition of who is considered a "criminal".

A "criminal", under Mr. Trump's new order, is anyone who has been charged with a criminal offense, even if it has not led to a conviction. It also includes anyone who has "committed acts that constitute a chargeable criminal offense," which means anyone authorities believe has broken any type of law — regardless of whether that person has been charged with a crime.

This order also encompasses anyone who has engaged in "fraud or willful misrepresentation in connection with any official matter or application before a governmental agency," a category that includes anyone who has ever used a false Social Security number to obtain a job, a common practice of unauthorized immigrants.

This is patently unconstitutional as everyone in the US is entitled to due process which determines that one is innocent until proven guilty.

Just hours after Trump signed his executive order expanding the definition of "criminal", Guadalupe Garcia de Rayos, a 35-year old Mexican mother of two US citizens who has lived in the US since she was 14, went to the Immigration and Customs Enforcement (ICE) local office in Arizona for her annual routine check-in, her eighth visit to ICE since her 2008 arrest and conviction for using a fake Social Security number.

In all her previous annual check-ins, Guadalupe would be released and would return back to her family. Not this time. After Trump's order went into effect, Guadalupe was detained and deported back to her native Mexico within 24 hours.

In an interview in Nogales, Mexico, Guadalupe told reporters that she had feared what might happen if she reported to ICE. An immigrants' rights group advised her to skip the check-in and go into hiding or seek refuge at a sanctuary church in North Phoenix.

Before her fateful appointment with ICE, Guadalupe and her family attended Mass. She said she clasped her hands and bowed her head in prayer and asked God to protect her.

[It would be curious to be a fly in the sky when Guadalupe meets her Maker and expresses her disappointment that God didn't protect her when she needed Him. God would reply that He sent an immigrants' rights group to warn her not to go to her ICE appointment and to seek sanctuary in a church instead but she ignored them. What can God do?]

HOW MANY TNTs?

The total estimate of "deportable aliens" living in the US is anywhere from a low of 11 million to the high estimate of 30 million given by right-wing Trump supporter Ann Coulter.

"The number we keep hearing is 11 million, 11 million, 11 million. That's so weird. It's been 11 million for a decade. But as I explain in the book, they are all using the Census figures. If the Census figures are wrong, then everybody's numbers are wrong," Coulter insisted in an interview with Univision's Jorge Ramos.

The estimate of Filipino TNTs in the US also varies from the low official estimate of 271,000 offered by Philippine Secretary of Labor Silvestre Bello to a high of 1 million given by Bernadette Ellorin, chair of Bayan USA.

"One out of every four Filipinos in the US is undocumented. That's approximately 1 million TNTs living in the shadows and in fear of a repressive Trump administration that has called Filipinos 'animals' and from a 'terrorist' nation," Ellorin said.

Special envoy to the U.S. Jose Manuel "Babe" Romualdez told CNN Philippines recently that the US Department of Homeland Security (DHS) identified "310,000 Filipinos up for deportation" but, he said, the number could be higher. An estimated four million Filipinos are living in the U.S. Romualdez said that of this number, 800,000 could be "illegals".

Romualdez advised the TNTs to return to the Philippines before they are deported, advice contrary to what the Mexican government plans to do to assist its nationals in the United States.

THE EXAMPLE OF MEXICO

Immediately after Trump's election, Mexico's Foreign Minister Claudia Ruiz Massieu vowed to draw up "plans of consular protection and assistance" for the millions of her countrymen facing imminent removal from the US under a president who has called them "murderers and rapists".

Massieu spoke directly to Mexicans living in the United States through a video feed on Twitter. "Countrymen, these are moments of uncertainty," she said. "Be calm, do not fall for provocations, and don't let yourself be fooled."

She explained that the Mexican government plans to strengthen its ties with officials at the state and local level who can ensure local regulations are in place to protect Mexican communities there. Mexico also plans to strengthen ties with nongovernmental civic organizations that support the Mexican community.

Mexico will also expand its consular services like providing government IDs to undocumented immigrants, helping immigrants find their birth certificates, and providing general legal assistance. It will launch a new toll-free number and roll out an app for Mexicans to use if they need any kind of assistance.

In contrast to Mexico's posture, Philippine President Rodrigo Duterte announced that undocumented Filipinos facing deportation from America due to US President Donald Trump's crackdown on illegal immigrants and refugees cannot expect help from the Duterte administration.

"To Filipinos there (in the United States), you better be on the right track. If you are not allowed to stay there where you are staying, get out because if you are caught and deported, I will not lift a finger. You know that it is a violation of the law," Duterte said in a press conference.

Duterte said he would respect Trump's executive action because Trump had assured him that he too would respect Duterte's brutal war on drugs in the Philippines. Quid pro quo.

"If he has policies to protect his country, I will understand … So out of respect, I will not interfere," Mr. Duterte said.

The TNTs remit billions of dollars to their families in the Philippines even as they live in hovels and are regularly subject to abuse by employers who take advantage of their "illegal" status by paying them low wages and long hours.

With Duterte as president, Filipino TNTs cannot expect their government to "lift a finger" to help them except a middle finger to tell them they're on their own.

They will have to rely on their families and friends and on the network of non-governmental organizations (NGOs) in the Filipino American community.

A UNITED FIL-AM COMMUNITY

Two days after Trump issued his anti-immigrant executive orders, the Filipino community in Jersey City, New Jersey held a town hall meeting at the Philippine Community Center to discuss the orders' impact on them.

Atty. Cristina Godinez of the Migrant Center at the Church of St. Francis of Assisi said: "The two EOs are just the beginning. They are un-American not just because they go against the proud history of the US as a nation of immigrants. These EOs pose a national security risk because they drive the undocumented deeper into the shadows. Non-citizens who had or will have any encounter with law enforcement—no matter how minor—are at risk," warned Godinez.

"The EOs' language is so broad that this Trump dragnet will potentially capture TNTs, those who are here as tourists, students or temporary workers, and even green card holders most of whom are peaceful, productive members of our communities," added Godinez.

The National Federation of Filipino American Associations (NaFFAA), with 12 regional chapters throughout the US (naffaa.org), held a Board Summit of its national Board of Governors in Houston, Texas on January 27-28, 2017 to address this issue among many other pressing matters.

Speaking for a united Board, NaFFAA National Chair Brendan Flores said, "We are closely monitoring President Trump's recent executive orders, which has the potential to affect many lives of Filipino-Americans, including refugees and immigrant families across the nation. The United States has always been a nation of immigrants, and a beacon of democracy. NaFFAA is committed to work with other Filipino American leaders and advocacy groups to uphold our country's cherished values during these transitional times."

NaFFAA Executive Director Jason Tengco added: "We cannot overlook the fact that during his campaign, then-candidate Trump suggested banning immigration from certain countries, including the Philippines. NaFFAA wants to serve as a forum for Filipino Americans to work together to ensure that community members are aware and engaged moving forward."

One positive outcome of Trump's anti-immigrant putsch is that groups from all political stripes in the Fil-Am community are coming together to unite on this issue. The National Alliance for Filipino Concerns (NAFCON) and Migrante SOMA held a town hall meeting at the Bayanihan Community Center in San Francisco to discuss the dire situation of TNTs who, they said, "live in a perpetual state of fear and uncertainty."

"They shouldn't live in fear," said Terrence Valen, director of Filipino Community Center and president of NAFCON. "They should be prepared, and assert their rights together with community groups and organizations. Lawyers are ready and willing to help them."

Princess R. Bustos, a community organizer for Migrante SoMa added: "We are our only defense, and the only way that we can fight against these attacks against our community is to stand together, fight for our rights, and protect each other," she said. "We will not let Trump's divisive tactics of pitting groups against each stray us from holding him accountable."

Though Duterte and his government will not lift a finger to help Filipino TNTs in the US, the Filipino American community promises to use all the fingers in all their hands to band them all together to protect and support our TNTs.

By pulling together, TNT should also now stand for "*Tulong nang Tulong*". Always helping. *(Send comments to Rodel50@gmail.com or mail them to the Law Offices of Rodel Rodis at 2429 Ocean Avenue, San Francisco, CA 94127 or call 415.334.7800).*

ooooo

3
Duterte Won't Declare Martial Law;
He Doesn't Have To
Nov. 15, 2016

I am absolutely confident that Pres. Rodrigo Duterte will not declare martial law. This confidence is based on the bountiful evidence that the Filipino people seem entirely too willing to voluntarily surrender their fundamental constitutional rights so there would be no need to formally declare martial law.

This conclusion is drawn from the public reaction to a speech Pres. Duterte delivered at the regional convention of the Integrated Bar of the Philippines (IBP) on November 4. In that Manila Hotel speech, Duterte informed his audience of lawyers that there will be a massive demonstration against him in the United States next year and that the moving force behind this protest is Filipino American Loida Nicolas-Lewis.

"Meron next year, a certain financier, mayaman na babae who married a black and is now a millionaire and she is planning to do massive demonstration," he said.

An online publication, politics.com.ph reported Duterte's speech in its November 4, 2016 issue with this sensationalized banner headline: "**Duterte unmasks Loida Nicolas Lewis' plot to launch massive protests to oust him.**"

If that report is true, is that a crime? If not, why did Duterte feel the need to "unmask" Loida?

IS ORGANIZING A PROTEST RALLY A CRIME?

The Philippine lawyers at that convention, as well as Duterte himself, who was a former government prosecutor, are all aware of Article III Section 4 of the 1987 Philippine Constitution which states that "No law shall be passed abridging the freedom of speech, of expression, or of the press, or the right of the people peaceably to assemble and petition the government for redress of grievances".

The IBP members are also familiar with the Philippine case of <u>Jacinto vs. Court of Appeal</u> [346 SCRA 665 (1997)] which held that the right to peaceably assemble and petition for redress of grievances is, together with freedom of speech, of expression and of the press, "a right that enjoy primacy in the realm of constitutional protection. For these rights constitute the very basis of a functional democratic policy, without which all the other rights would be meaningless and unprotected."

But yet none of the Philippine lawyers at the Manila Hotel on Nov. 4 stood up to defend Loida Nicolas Lewis, who placed 7th in the Philippine bar exams in 1967, and who was the first Filipina to be admitted to practice law in New York state. None dared to assert to Pres. Duterte that Loida has every right to call for a peaceful demonstration against Duterte even if it is "massive".

One Philippine attorney stood up for Loida. In his Internet post, former senator Rene

Saguisag wrote that he has known Loida since the early 1960s when they were both involved in the Student Catholic Action (SCA) and in the National Union of Students (NUS) and when they "bar-reviewed" together in San Beda in 1967 although Loida went to the University of the Philippines School of Law.

"I know that if Loida wants something done," Saguisag wrote, "she will do it by the force of reason and never by reason of force. She'll do it morally and legally… No mean bone in a kind and gentle soul."

Saguisag expressed concern that a few of Duterte's followers may be "unhinged" and that therefore "Loida needs to be more careful here, where she spends a lot of time, doing good, or elsewhere." The former senator wondered "how the lawyers in that Integrated Bar of the Philippines assembly responded when the Prez, willy-nilly, casually put lawyer Loida's safety in jeopardy, by convicting her by publicity."

"We have to have a higher regard for human life and dignity," Saguisag counselled.

CAUSE FOR SAGUISAG'S CONCERN

There is good reason for Saguisag to be concerned for Loida's safety. After Duterte's attack against Loida appeared online, Duterte's numerous supporters in the social media immediately began trolling Loida in their Facebook pages.

One such Duterte supporter, Mira Savaria Encabo, an OFW based in Bahrain, posted this Facebook blast against Loida Nicolas Lewis:

"She is the Mouthpiece of America but posturing a facade of Filipino patriot. How can she be a pro-Filipino when all her businesses are in the US and all her allegiance is to the American flag??? Can we let a Fil-Am whose only claim to fame is her being married to a rich African-American and who doesn't even have the guts to bring or donate even a little portion of her wealth and money to Philippines to help the government and the poor???

What had she done to help the country and have the guts to organize a destabilization move and to OUST THE BEST PRESIDENT PHILIPPINES EVER HAD IN THE RECENT HISTORY???? ALL SHE DID IS TALKING TOO MUCH and going for TV INTERVIEWS! Pretending to be the voice of the people!!!

What right does she have to meddle in Philippine affairs when she lives comfortably in US, sheltered from all the trappings of life in the Philippines while she enjoys the luxury of her late husband's wealth????

Why can't she concentrate campaigning against discrimination and racism which the blacks are still experiencing in US? It would definitely make her late husband's soul to rejoice knowing his money is being spent in something worth fighting for rather than spending it trying to demoralize, destabilize and throw out the government and PRESIDENCY LEGALLY ELECTED by the PEOPLE!!!"

It is evident that the Duterte supporter never bothered to google search "Loida Nicolas Lewis" and relied entirely on Duterte's false description of her as simply "mayaman na babae who married a black and is now a millionaire."

THE TRUTH ABOUT LOIDA NICOLAS LEWIS

If any of them had bothered to do basic research, they would have learned that Loida was already a lawyer when she met Reginald F. Lewis (not "Richard") on a blind date in New York City in 1968 when he graduated from Harvard Law School, and that they were married a year later in Manila.

They lived in a condo in Manhattan while raising their two daughters with Loida employed as a lawyer for the Immigration and Naturalization Service (INS) while Reginald was working for a top New York law firm. After 15 years as a corporate lawyer, Reginald formed his own venture capital firm in 1983, TLC Group L.P., which he then used to purchase Beatrice International Foods in 1987 which became the first black-owned company to have more than $1 billion in annual sales.

In 1993, Reginald Lewis died of cerebral hemorrhage from brain cancer. A year later, Loida was picked by the Board of Directors to be the CEO and chair of the board of TLC Beatrice, a post she held until 2000. As CEO, she cut costs and sold non-core and under-performing assets, reduced liabilities and strengthened the management team. In October 1995, Loida was named the top US business executive by the

National Foundation for Women Business Owners and Working Woman Magazine.

Also, contrary to the misinformation being spread on social media by Duterte supporters, Loida has invested heavily in the Philippines including founding and operating The Lewis College in Sorsogon which offers quality education in accountancy and business as well as in science and technology, providing scholarships to the poor students of her home province of Sorsogon.

As chair of US Pinoys for Good Governance, Loida Nicolas Lewis, a dual citizen of the US and the Philippines, has also championed the cause of Philippine sovereignty in the West Philippine Sea leading global protests against the Chinese invasion in Philippine territorial waters. She has called for a global boycott of goods made in China making her "China's Public Enemy #1".

The malicious attacks on Loida Nicolas Lewis by Duterte on November 4 were not aimed at just silencing Loida but were directed at discouraging Filipino Americans from joining protest demonstrations against his administration.

THE MESSAGE FOR FILIPINOS IN THE PHILIPPINES

For the Filipinos in the Philippines, the message was delivered the following day on November 5 when more than a dozen fully-armed members of the Criminal Investigation and Detection Group of Eastern Visayas (CIDG-8) arrived at the provincial jail cell of Albuera, Leyte Mayor Rolando Espinosa at around 4 a.m.

"to serve a search warrant" on him. They removed all the jail guards and proceeded to shoot and kill Espinosa and his cell mate.

Columnist Solita Monsod described the police officers' cover story as "so flimsy it was evident that the police were confident that they would get away with it."

Sure enough, a week later, Duterte announced that he believed the version of events presented by the police, whatever it is, as incredible as it may be. Duterte reiterated his promise to protect cops from being charged if the cases filed against them came while they were doing their duty.

As Rigoberto Tiglao commented in his Manila Times column on November 13, 2016: "Duterte's stance means we no longer have a rule of law in this country but the rule of a President and his police who can execute anybody they want, and claim that their target had fought it out and the police didn't have any choice but to defend themselves."

"The CIDG-8 demonstrated how the police can undertake such execution with total impunity and brazenness that we should all be outraged, not only at such trampling of our rule of law, but at such ruthless, merciless murder carried out by supposed agents of the law," Tiglao wrote.

So, it's good news, bad news. The good news is that Pres. Duterte will not declare martial law. The bad news is that no one would notice it now if he did.

ooooo

4

Dissing God, Cussing Obama and Praising Hitler - What a Week

Oct. 7, 2016

President Duterte's mouth set a new world record for traveling the longest distance in the shortest time. In a span of just six days, it traveled from doubting God in Heaven to condemning Obama to Hell and they were not even the most offensive remarks uttered in that week.

Speaking before journalists in Malacanang Palace on September 27, 2016, Duterte justified the restoration of the death penalty as necessary to "make up for divine inconsistency". (*Duterte: I can teach God about justice*"). In his speech, Duterte criticized the "bleeding hearts" in the Catholic Church for their opposition to the death penalty because of their belief that "only God can kill". Duterte said he did not want to have to wait until Judgment Day. "What if there is no God?" he asked.

Six days later, in an October 3 speech to local officials, Duterte complained that the United States was refusing to sell weapons to his government and, therefore, President Obama "can go to hell." He had been angered by Washington's criticism of his take-no-prisoners crusade against drug addicts and he threatened to turn to China and Russia for weapons purchases.

Duterte may not realize that the funds used by the Philippines to purchase weapons from the US come from US military assistance ($340 million since 2001) and they can only be used to purchase US arms, not arms from Russia or China.

THE LEAHY LAW

Contrary to Duterte's assumption, Pres. Obama's refusal to authorize the Philippine purchase of US arms was not to get back at him for his "son of a whore" insult, but to comply with the Leahy Law, named after principal sponsor Sen. Patrick Leahy of Vermont, which prohibits the U.S. Department of State and Department of Defense from providing military assistance to foreign military units that violate human rights with impunity.

In the same week that Duterte had cussed Obama, Sen. Leahy denounced Duterte on the floor of the US Senate for "advocating and endorsing what amounts to mass murder." Sen. Ben Cardin of Maryland echoed Leahy's sentiment: "Senator Leahy is absolutely right when he said that a lack of respect for rule of law and democratic governance breeds instability, distrust, and sometimes violence."

Obama has no choice but to comply with the "rule of law", the Leahy Law, a problem that doesn't exist for the despots in Russia or China.

There is a way to get around the Leahy Law, as US Major General Paul Eaton explained: "The value of the Leahy Law is that it serves as a moral guide to the application of U.S. military engagement. Some in the U.S. armed forces have argued that the law frustrates U.S. partnership at precisely the moment we need most to influence better behaviors. This dilemma has a solution embedded in the amendment itself, which provides that if human rights remediation has begun, U.S. assistance can be brought to bear."

Unfortunately, human rights "remediation" is not likely to happen any time soon under Duterte. In fact, it may only get exponentially worse.

"HAPPY TO SLAUGHTER THEM"

On September 30, after arriving back in Manila from a brief official visit to Vietnam, Duterte complained that he had been "portrayed or pictured to be a cousin of Hitler."

Rather than objecting to it, Duterte reveled in the comparison. "Hitler massacred 3 million Jews ... there's 3 million drug addicts," he said. "There are. I'd be happy to slaughter them."

Duterte's newly appointed Philippine Ambassador to the United Nations, Teddyboy Locsin, Jr, posted a tweet in support of his boss: "I believe that the Drug Menace is so big it needs a FINAL SOLUTION like the Nazis adopted. That I believe. NO REHAB."

The pushback was immediate. German Foreign Ministry spokesman Martin Schaefer denounced Duterte's comments as "unacceptable" stating: "It is impossible to make any comparison to the unique atrocities of the Shoah and Holocaust."

World Jewish Congress President Ronald Lauder said Duterte's remarks were "revolting" and added: "Drug abuse is a serious issue. But what President Duterte said is not only profoundly inhumane, but it demonstrates an appalling disrespect for human life that is truly heartbreaking for the democratically elected leader of a great country."

Rep. Teodoro Baguilat asked Duterte if his policy means that "it's open season now for all addicts, no more rehabilitation, just kill them systematically like what the Nazis did with the Jews."

Duterte was not content to just happily slaughter 3 million drug addicts in the Philippines, he even sought to export his kill-the-drug-addicts policy to Indonesia.

After he attended the ASEAN conference in Laos, Duterte visited Indonesia where the country's anti-drugs chief, Budi Waseso, held a press conference declaring that Indonesia would launch a Duterte-style drug purge. Later, however, a spokesman for the national narcotics agency clarified that Indonesian "punishments have to be in accordance with our law and with national and international standards."

REHABILITATION FOR DRUG ADDICTS

Indonesia is evaluating its treatment of drug addicts. In an article in The Jakarta Post on March 20, 2014 ("Should drug addicts be jailed or rehabilitated?"), Kartono Mohamad, the chairman of the Indonesian Public Health Scholars Association, wrote that "the idea of treating drug users as criminals came from the fact they use or are in possession of drugs, which by law are declared illegal…On the other hand, drug addiction is also considered a form of social disease, like prostitution. Not so long ago HIV was also regarded a social disease. That is why Law No. 35/2009 on narcotics and addictive drugs provides treatment and rehabilitation for drug addicts, but not for drug traffickers or dealers."

"In that case, we are inclined to differentiate between those who intentionally hook other people to become addicts and those who are the victim of the former group. Here starts the idea of treating drug addicts as victims. As victims they deserve empathy, treatment and assistance to get rid of their addiction through rehabilitation."

The same reevaluation of the treatment of drug addicts is taking place in the United Arab Emirates where Sheikh Saif bin Zayed, the Minister of Interior and Deputy Prime Minister, had ordered all concerned authorities to evaluate current anti-drugs laws and suggest reforms.

Brig Gen Maktoum al Sharifi, the head of the Abu Dhabi Capital Police, welcomed the idea of reforms, saying the law should not consider a drug offender a criminal, as it currently does.

"A drug addict is a sick person and he should be treated as such," Brig Gen al Sharifi said. "Alternative punishment would be more effective. A drug offender could be just an addict, not a criminal, but after locking him up for years he could come out involved in crimes such as stealing, drug dealing, et cetera." The Abu Dhabi Police has proposed alternative punishments which include community service, such as cleaning the streets, schools or voluntary work.

"I WILL KILL THREE MILLION"

To cap a strange week, Duterte visited a Jewish Synagogue in Manila on Sunday October 2 to apologize to the Jewish people for his remarks. In a speech that was televised nationally, he explained that his comments were a reaction to negative criticism. "So I said, 'Sure, I am Hitler, but the ones I will kill are these drug addicts ... but it is not really that I said something wrong. But rather, they do not really want to tinker with the memory so I apologize profoundly and deeply to the Jewish people."

http://www.dw.com/en/philippine-president-duterte-apologizes-for-pro-hitler-comments/a-35943457

"I would like to make it clear, here and now, that there was never an intention on my part to derogate the memory of six million Jews murdered. The reference to me was, I was supposedly Hitler, who killed many people ... But I was very emphatic. I will kill three million," he said.

And then he unloaded again:: "The Americans, I don't like them ... they are reprimanding me in public. So I say: 'Screw you, f--k you, everything else. You are stupid."

And that's how President Duterte ended his week.

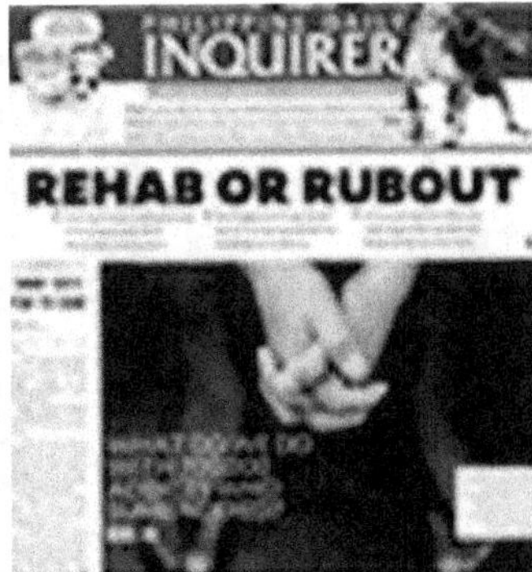

Ooooo

5

A Trump Presidency and the Consequences for Filipinos

Aug. 5, 2016

On the 74th anniversary of the bombing of Pearl Harbor, Republican presidential nominee Donald J. Trump dropped what the *London Daily Telegraph* called a "bombshell" when he announced that if elected president of the United States, he would implement a "total and complete shutdown of Muslims entering the United States."

Trump's campaign manager at the time Corey Lewandowski explained that Trump's proposed ban would apply to "everybody," including Muslims seeking immigrant visas as well as tourists seeking to enter the country. The ban would even apply to American Muslims who are currently overseas – presumably including members of the military and diplomatic service, another Trump staffer added.

Trump's proposed Muslim ban drew outrage from leaders in Asia who warned that Trump was helping the cause of ISIS by feeding Islamic State propaganda that depicted a grand war between Islam and the West.

"By uttering such a hate-spreading statement, Donald Trump has committed a crime by indirectly helping the cause of so-called global Islamist militants such as Islamic State," the chairman of the Jamiatul Ulama Bangladesh, an Islamic scholars council, told the press.

No PH reaction

But there was no outcry from Philippine officials or civil society that this bigoted policy would harm the 15 percent of the Philippine population that is Muslim. Were Filipino Christians willing to throw their Muslim brothers and sisters under the Trump bus?

Even the Filipino American community remained painfully silent on this issue. I confess that I too did not denounce Trump and his xenophobic bigotry in my columns published in the US and in the Philippines. I was content to just post my revulsion with Trump in my Facebook page.

In Indonesia, the world's most populous Muslim nation, Zuhairi Misrawi, an Islamic scholar from Muslim organization Nahdlatul Ulama, said the call was "a step backwards" for America. "We previously regarded America as a role model for democracy, equality, peace and justice," he said.

Trump's proposed Muslim ban relies on a US law that grants the president the authority to issue executive orders to prevent the entry of any class of people who would be considered "detrimental to the interests of the United States."

Detrimental to the interests of the United States? Sen. Lindsey Graham (R-South Carolina) pointed out that Trump's comments are "hurting the war effort and putting our diplomats and soldiers serving in the Middle East at risk. The way to win this war is to reach to the vast majority of people in Islamic faith who reject ISIS and provide them the capability to resist this ideology."

Perhaps in response to severe criticism from fellow Republicans about his religious intolerance, Trump modified his position so it would not expressly ban Muslims simply because of their faith. In his acceptance speech on July 21, Trump announced that he would now ban immigration from countries "compromised by terrorism."

Without mentioning the word "Muslim," Trump said: "We must immediately suspend immigration from any nation that has been compromised by terrorism until such time as proven vetting mechanisms have been put in place," Trump said. "We don't want them in our country."

When pressed by Meet the Press TV host Chuck Todd about whether his ban on immigration from countries "compromised by terrorism" would include countries like France and Belgium which have suffered terrorist attacks in recent years, Trump declined to answer. Instead, he replied, "It's their own fault, because they've allowed people over years to come into their territory."

Guess which country in Southeast Asia has been most "compromised by terrorism"?

PH 'compromised by terrorism'?

Aside from Indonesia, with its Jamiyah Islamiyah militants, the Philippines would also be high on the list with its own homegrown terrorists, Abu Sayyaf, which is based in Sulu and Basilan in Mindanao. The Abus have waged a brutal campaign of bombings, kidnappings and assassinations, killing Filipinos and foreign nationals since their founding in 1991, as an offshoot of the Moro National Liberation Front. In 2004, they claimed responsibility for the bombing of Superferry 14 killing 116 people.

In 2014, the Abu Sayyaf, led by its leader, Isnilon Totoni Hapilon, pledged its loyalty to Abu Bakr al-Baghdadi, the leader of ISIS. Since then, it has been kidnapping foreigners for ransom and mercilessly beheading them if its demands are not met.

So if Trump is elected president, Philippine tourists may be barred from entering the US even for those with US relatives who are diehard Republicans who voted for Trump. Filipinos don't even have to be Muslim to be barred from entry as long as the Philippines is deemed a country "compromised by terrorism." The rest of the Philippines would now be included along with the 15 percent Muslim that would be thrown under the Trump bus. United at last.

As Trump would say, "It's their fault, they've allowed (Muslims) over the years to come into their territory." Of course, Muslims have lived in the Philippines since before the Spaniards came. In fact, Manila was a Muslim settlement under Rajah Soliman (Suleyman) when the Spaniards invaded it in 1565.

We can't ignore it now, can we?

Abu Sayyaf terrorist band. INQUIRER FILE

There is another Trump campaign promise that would also dramatically affect Filipinos. Trump has vowed to deport an estimated 11.3 million "illegal immigrants" in the US. Many believe the actual number to be much higher, at least 15 million. Although the emphasis in the media has focused mostly on Latinos who crossed the border from Mexico, the list includes probably 500,000 Filipinos, those affectionately called TNTs ("*tago nang tago*" – always hiding).

Trump would deport 500K Filipinos

Experts posit that it would take 20 years to remove "illegals" or "undocumented" aliens from the US, an estimate provided by the American Action Forum (AAF), a conservative think tank that released a 2015 study that showed that it would require 650 busloads every month for two decades. The total cost of a 20-year mass deportation program would be about $600 billion.

The AAF Report also conservatively estimated that "illegals" make up about 6.4 percent of the US labor force – about 11 million in 2014. Deporting them would shrink the US economy by nearly 6 percent or $1.6 trillion by 2035.

Many of the TNTs who would be deported by a President Trump have lived in the US for more than 20 years, are working in low-paying jobs, and regularly remit money to their relatives in the Philippines.

Of the $25 billion a year in overseas Filipino remittances to the Philippines, about 45 percent comes from the US and a large proportion of these funds comes from TNTs. Their deportation from the US would devastate the Philippine economy.

Filipino American voters in the November elections in the US should realize the political consequences of their vote.

ooooo

6
Comparing Dr. Jose Rizal and Ninoy Aquino
Dateline, 2015

In all of Philippine history, no two national heroes were as similar in how they lived and in how they died than Dr. Jose Rizal and Benigno "Ninoy" Aquino Jr., whose 32nd death anniversary we commemorate this week.

Both came from similar class backgrounds. Their families were just below hacendero level landed gentry; both studied at the elite Ateneo school; both traveled extensively, wrote prolifically, and returned to the Philippines from safety abroad despite warnings that they faced certain death upon setting foot on native soil.

Both were tried on sham charges by kangaroo courts which sentenced them to death. Both were executed by Filipino soldiers following the orders of the powerful forces who feared their return. Each of their deaths sparked revolutions that overthrew the tyrannies that caused their martyrdoms.

Rizal and Aquino both fit the textbook model of a "tragic hero" - born of privilege, imbued with heroic qualities, and fated to endure great suffering. In the classic mold, Prof. Ronald Santora relates, "the hero struggles mightily against this fate and this cosmic conflict wins our admiration."

Why did Dr. Jose Rizal in 1892 and Ninoy Aquino in 1983 return to the Philippines knowing of the certain death that awaited them upon their arrival? Was it fate or free will?

Dr. Jose Rizal lived and studied in Europe for almost a decade, obtaining advanced degrees in fine arts, medicine (ophthalmology), and even a doctorate in languages. Rizal also wrote two novels, Noli Mi Tangere and El Filibusterismo, which exposed Spanish abuses in the Philippines.

Aside from his academic achievements, Rizal also immersed himself in the Filipino expatriate movement for reforms, organizing forums and contributing regular editorial essays to the movement's main journal, La Solidaridad.

On November 20, 1891, Rizal moved to Hong Kong and established a private practice in ophthalmology which drew patients from throughout the crown colony. Before the end of the year, Rizal was able to get his parents and siblings to live with him in a comfortable home in Hong Kong.

While Rizal was overjoyed to be finally reunited with his family, he was deeply dismayed by the factionalism and lack of unity that plagued the Filipino expatriate movement in Europe. As Jose Baron Fernandez noted in his book, (Jose Rizal: Filipino Doctor and Patriot, 1980):

"During the first two months in 1892, the propaganda campaign was in disarray; (Marcelo) Del Pilar in Madrid, abandoned by all except his brother-in-law, (Graciano) Lopez-Jaena in Barcelona, very skeptical of La Propaganda, with its utter neglect of its obligations, and, finally, the new committee of La Propaganda which proposed to Rizal the launching of a new fortnightly paper, as well as the organization of a new party "the Rizalist party". Meanwhile, from Paris came news of the formation of a revolutionary organization called Katipunan (headed by Andres Bonifacio)".

Ninoy Aquino had been incarcerated in solitary confinement by the dictator Ferdinand Marcos for almost eight years by May of 1980, when he suffered two severe heart attacks within a week of each other. Because of fear of negative publicity if Aquino died while under military custody, First Lady Imelda Marcos ordered him released and quickly flown to the US on May 9, 1980. The conjugal dictators expected him to die on an operating table at a hospital in Dallas, Texas, but Aquino somehow defied the odds and survived.

After recuperating from heart surgery, Aquino spent three years in the US, setting up a home in the Boston suburb of Newton, Massachusetts together with two future Philippine presidents, his wife, Cory, and son, Noynoy, and their other children. Ninoy received fellowship grants from Harvard University and the Massachusetts Institute of Technology, worked on the manuscripts of two books, and delivered speeches throughout the US denouncing Marcos and martial law.

Aquino also found himself caught in the factional intrigues of the anti-Marcos opposition in the US. On the rght flank was the Movement for a Free Philippines (MFP) under Sen. Raul Manglapus which advocated for the return of parliamentary democracy. On the left was the Katipunan ng mga Demokratikong Pilipino (KDP or Union of Democratic Filipinos) which supported the revolutionary overthrow of the Marcos dictatorship.

In the first quarter of 1983, Aquino received disturbing news of the deteriorating political situation in the Philippines with the consensus belief that the Philippines was just five years away from a full-scale bloody Communist revolution. Because of the declining health of Marcos, Aquino felt it imperative to return to the Philippines to convince Marcos to restore democracy "before extremists take over and make such a change impossible".

Like Aquino, Rizal too feared the very revolution his own writings had inspired. "Rizal was opposed to Bonifacio's revolution," writer-historian F. Sionil Jose explained. "To seek his support, Pio Valenzuela visited him in Dapitan where the Spaniards had exiled him. Rizal argued that Filipinos were not ready for a revolution, that the cost and the bloodshed would be tremendous.

Seeking to avert bloody revolutions, both freely chose to return back to the Philippines to personally make the case for a non-violent reform alternative. But their pleas fell on deaf ears. Rizal was executed in Luneta (now Rizal Park) on December 30, 1896 by a firing squad of Filipino soldiers acting on the orders of Malacanang Palace. Ninoy was killed at the tarmac of the Manila International Airport (now the Ninoy Aquino International Airport) on August 21, 1983 by an execution squad of Filipino soldiers acting also on the orders of Malacanang Palace.

Just before returning to the Philippines, Rizal wrote a letter to the Filipino people dated 20 June 1892 where he explained:

"The step I have taken or am about to take is very risky no doubt and I do not have to say that I have given it much thought. I know that almost everyone is against it but I know too that almost no one knows what goes in my heart. I cannot go on living knowing that so many suffer unjust persecution because of me … I also want to show those who deny our patriotism that we know how to die doing our duty and for our convictions. What does death matter if one dies for what one loves, for one's country and loved ones?"

In the statement he planned to read upon his arrival at the Manila airport, Aquino wrote:

"I have returned on my free will to join the ranks of those struggling to restore our rights and freedoms through nonviolence. I seek no confrontation. I only pray and will strive for a genuine national reconciliation founded on justice. I am prepared for the worst, and have decided against the advice of my mother, my spiritual adviser, many of my tested friends and a few of my most valued political mentors. A death sentence awaits me...but I feel it is my duty, as it is the duty of every Filipino, to suffer with his people especially in time of crisis. I never sought nor have I been given assurances or promise of leniency by the regime. I return voluntarily armed only with a clear conscience and fortified in the faith that in the end justice will emerge triumphant. According to Gandhi, the willing sacrifice of the innocent is the most powerful answer to insolent tyranny that has yet been conceived by God and man."

Rizal's execution triggered the Katipunan revolution that led to the Filipino people's overthrow of Spanish rule. Ninoy's execution sparked the People Power revolution that led to the overthrow of Marcos rule.

In their cosmic conflicts against their fates, by their words and by their deeds, Dr. Jose Rizal and Ninoy Aquino transformed the Philippines and the Filipino people.

ooooo

7

Global Networking: What PH can teach Americas about proper treatment of Syrian refugees

Dec. 4, 2016

One week after the ISIS terrorist attack in Paris, the Republican-dominated US House of Representatives passed a bill to halt the admission of Syrian refugees into the U.S. until they undergo a "more stringent vetting process," one that virtually assures that no Syrian refugee will be allowed to enter the US.

Not to be outdone by the action of their colleagues in the House, the nation's Republican governors announced that their states will not accept Syrian refugees.

With these actions, the Republicans have sent the clear message to the world that "Syrian refugees are not welcome" in the US, a message that ironically falls in lockstep with the ISIS goal that targets the Syrian refugees. As Zach Beauchamp explained:

"ISIS despises Syrian refugees: It sees them as traitors to the caliphate. By leaving, they turn their backs on the caliphate. ISIS depicts its territory as a paradise, and fleeing refugees expose that as a lie. But if refugees do make it out, ISIS wants them to be treated badly -- the more the West treats them with suspicion and fear, the more it supports ISIS's narrative of a West that is hostile to Muslims and bolsters ISIS's efforts to recruit from migrant communities in Europe.

In sharp contrast to the actions of the Republicans, French President Francois Hollande declared that his country would still accept 30,000 Syrian refugees, an announcement at a gathering of French mayors that drew a standing ovation.

Hollande asserted that it was France's "humanitarian duty" to honor its commitments to Syrian refugees, even in the wake of the ISIS terror attacks which killed at least 129 people in Paris.

JEWISH REFUGEES BARRED IN US in 1939

Before the House voted on November 19, Rep. Jerrold Nadler (D-NY) reminded House members that "we face a choice that will echo through history" specifically referring to the time when the U.S. also turned away Jewish refugees fleeing Nazi Germany in 1939. "We must not let ourselves be guided by irrational fear."

What Rep. Nadler referred to was a 1939 incident that was made into a 1976 Hollywood film, *Voyage of the Damned*, which was based on the true story of the luxury liner MS St. Louis, which left Hamburg, Germany with 937 Jewish passengers bound for Florida where the US government refused to allow them to disembark. After the ship was refused entry in other ports, it returned to Germany where its Jewish passengers were forcibly removed and dispatched to concentration camps for extermination. A Nazi official in the film declares: "When the whole world has refused to accept them as refugees, no country can blame Germany for the fate of the Jews."

But at least one country can. In the year when the MS St. Louis was rejected by all the countries where it sought refuge, the Philippine Commonwealth accepted 1,300 Jewish refugees and was willing to accept as much as 10,000 more in Mindanao if the US State Department had allowed it to do so.

The Washington Times reported on December 5, 1938 (*"Quezon Urges Jews'Haven"*) that "the possibility of a haven for Jewish refugees from Germany was broached today by Pres. Manuel Quezon" who said "I am willing to facilitate entrance of such numbers of Jewish people as we could absorb…I favor large scale immigration to Mindanao, if well financed."

SAFE HAVEN FOR JEWISH REFUGEES

The Philippines has a proud history of being a haven for refugees seeking asylum, and of engaging in humanitarian efforts to resettle them. A refugee, as the United Nations defines it, is "any person who: owing to a well-founded fear of being persecuted for reasons of race, religion, nationality, membership of a particular social group, or political opinion, is outside the country of his nationality, and is unable to or, owing to such fear, is unwilling to avail himself of the protection of that country.

Syrian Refugees + Jewish Refugees

On February 15, 1939, Philippine Commonwealth Pres. Quezon said that this country "could not turn a deaf ear to the sufferings of these unfortunate people."

A year later, the Philippine Congress passed the Philippine Immigration Act of 1940 which provided Quezon with broad discretionary powers "to admit aliens who are refugees for religious, political, or racial reasons, in such classes of cases and under such conditions as he may prescribe."

On April 23, 1940, Quezon personally greeted 40 Jewish refugee families to the 8 hectares of land he had donated to them in Marikina saying in his welcome address:

"It is my hope, and indeed my expectation, that the people of the Philippines will have in the future every reason to be glad that when the time of need came, their country was willing to extend a hand of welcome.

CHINESE AND WHITE RUSSIAN REFUGEES

The Philippine welcome mat was not just extended to Jewish refugees. In 1937, when the Japanese Imperial Forces invaded mainland China, Quezon issued Proclamation No. 173 offering aid to refugees from China fleeing the Japanese invasion.

In December 1948, Pres. Elpidio Quirino offered refuge to 8,000 "White Russians", supporters of the Russian Tsar who had fled to Shanghai when the Bolsheviks seized power in 1922, and who then had to flee from China when the Chinese Communists defeated the Kuomintang. They were resettled in the former naval base of Tubabao Island in Guiuan, Samar.

INDOCHINESE REFUGEES

At the end of the Vietnam War in April of 1975, the Philippines opened its doors to thousands of Vietnamese and Cambodian refugees who were fleeing their countries by boat.

On August 21, 1979, the Philippines established a task force on international refugee assistance to work with the United Nations High Commission for Refugees (UNHCR) in giving aid to the refugees within its shores.

In its short history from April, 1975 to August, 1982, the Philippine Refugee Processing Center provided food, shelter and education to about 400, 000 Indochinese refugees.

"GREATEST COUNTRY IN THE WORLD"

In the HBO TV series, "Newsroom", lead anchorman Will McAvoy, portrayed by Jeff Daniels, is asked in a college forum "what makes America the greatest country in the world?" McAvoy hesitates before delivering the following:

"It's not the greatest country in the world, Professor, that's my answer…there's absolutely no evidence to support the statement that we're the greatest country in the world. We're 7th in literacy, 27th in math, 22nd in science, 49th in life expectancy, 178th in infant mortality, 3rd in median household income, number 4 in labor force and number 4 in exports. We lead the world in only three categories: Number of incarcerated citizens per capita, number of adults who believe angels are real, and defense spending where we spend more than the next 26 countries combined, 25 of whom are allies."

"It sure used to be. We stood up for what was right. We fought for moral reasons. We passed laws, struck down laws for moral reasons. We waged wars on poverty, not poor people. We sacrificed, we cared about our neighbors, we put our money where our mouths were and we never

beat our chests. We built great big things, made ungodly technological advances, explored the universe, cured diseases, and cultivated the world's greatest artists and the world's greatest economy. We reached for the stars, acted like men, we aspired to intelligence, we didn't belittle it, it didn't make us feel inferior."

The Philippines may be last in traffic management and in the integrity of its public officials but it is at least first in its humane and decent treatment of persecuted refugees.

ooooo

8

A Little Lesson in Political Empowerment

February 9, 2016

Filipinos in the U.S. who crave "political empowerment" may not know exactly what it means or how it affects them. In 1994, two years after I was elected to the San Francisco Community College Board (the first Filipino elected to public office in San Francisco), I was confronted with an issue that illustrates just exactly how it works.

As background, all 85 community college districts in California are governed by an elected 7-member Board. The San Francisco Community College Board oversees the City College of San Francisco which provides up to 110,000 students in ten campuses throughout the city with classes offering associate degrees, English as a Second Language (ESL), career and technical education, as well as lifelong learning courses.

FILIPINOS COMPRISE 10% OF CITY COLLEGE STUDENTS

In 1994, there were 3,850 Filipino students enrolled at the main Ocean campus of City College, coincidentally the same as the total number of African American students on campus, about 10% of the student population. To serve the needs of this large population, a Philippine Studies program was created in 1970 to offer more than a dozen courses (six per semester) on Philippine History, Philippine Society & Culture, the Filipino Family, Philippine Literature, Conversational Tagalog and other courses.

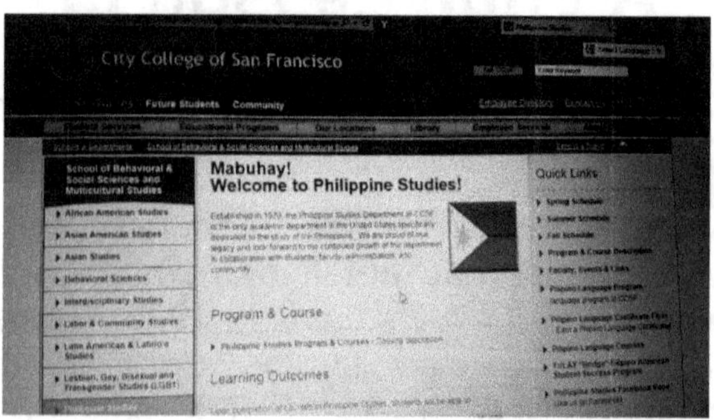

On January 14, 1991, the Philippine Studies Department hired Dr. Edwin Almirol as its department chair to teach three courses and run the department, developing other courses that could be offered in the future. Dr. Almirol was a highly regarded Ethnic Studies professor at the University of California at Davis who wrote "Rights and Obligations in Filipino American

Families" and other books focusing on the Filipino community.

With Dr. Almirol in charge, the Philippine Studies program was well on its way to sustained growth. Unfortunately, less than 2 years later, Dr. Almirol died quite unexpectedly. Because of a 5% cutback in state funding for City College, a hiring freeze was imposed on all faculty positions that had become vacant due to death or retirement. So Dr. Almirol could not be replaced with another instructor, which effectively eliminated half of the Philippine Studies courses offered.

ONLY 7 FULL TIME SLOTS

A year later, the Chancellor of City College announced that the state had restored 7 fulltime positions back to City College so we were hopeful that Philippine Studies would receive one of those slots. The problem is that there were 31 other full-time vacancies to fill in the various departments so Philippine Studies would have to compete with the traditional Math, English, Science, History departments as well as with the untraditional Lesbian Gay Bisexual Transgender (LGBT), La Raza, and Black studies departments that also needed to fill their vacancies.

Several Board meetings were scheduled to hear public testimony about which 7 vacancies would be filled. To prepare for the meeting where the Philippine Studies vacancy would be discussed, we contacted all the influential Fil-Am community leaders to speak, including then Philippine News publisher Alex Esclamado and California Fil Am Democratic Caucus founder Alice Bulos.

I would normally have been among those speaking and advocating for the Filipino community but I was then in the unaccustomed position of being among those who would decide the issue.

At the assigned date and time, our community speakers lined up at the podium and began to speak one after another about the injustice of denying Philippine Studies the full time position it sorely needed if it was to continue to stay afloat. The speakers presented the history of Filipinos in America as an oppressed community brought in as farm laborers to serve the needs of Hawaiian sugar planters and mainland growers in the 1920s, as stewards in the US Navy in the 40s and 50s, some who were part of the more than 200,000 Philippine Commonwealth soldiers conscripted into the US Army Forces in the Far East (USAFFE) in WW II, and as professionals who entered the U.S.

workforce after the liberalization of US immigration laws in 1965.

"We need to have our stories told so that the young generation of Filipinos will know our history and take pride in our culture and grow up with a positive image of being Filipinos," Alex Esclamado said.

KUNDIMAN APPROACH TO EMPOWERMENT

The speakers emphasized the damage that would be done to Philippine Studies at City College and to Philippine Studies programs around the US where the pioneering City College program is the model.

As they spoke, I began to hear the strains of Kundiman music in my head. "Kundiman", which is short for "kung hindi man" (if it is not to be), is the native Philippine music of unrequited love, of a love that is pure and chaste but is spurned. It was as if we were already preparing to be rejected.

I imagined in my head the pleas of centuries of tenant farmers in the Philippines tilling the land with their carabaos, planting rice, and harvesting the rice yields all year long only to give more than 90% of their produce to the obscenely rich landlords who own the land by inheritance and who rent it to them.

"Please, Senor Hacendero, please allow us to keep a few more bags of rice so that we can feed our families," they would beg on their hands and knees. "We've worked so hard for you, sir, we deserve to be given a break. Please sir."

I have heard this same type of plaintive cry whenever Filipinos ask for justice for Filipino WW II veterans who fought the Japanese invaders under the US flag but were denied promised U.S. citizenship and U.S. veterans benefits when their services were no longer needed after the war. The same plea was raised by aging Filipino farmworkers in Delano in the 1960s who were asking to be paid equally with the "bracero" Mexican workers. It was also the cry of elderly Manong residents of the International Hotel in the 1970s who were being evicted from their low cost hotel rooms to make way for Redevelopment.

A "WIN-WIN" APPROACH

I would have found nothing unusual about our kundiman way of expressing our "requests" to the people in power to please give us a break, because that was the way we have always done it. For centuries.

Except that I was also at the Board sessions of the other groups seeking to be awarded one of the coveted full time posts. I saw the stark difference in approach.

For example, when representatives of the LGBT community appeared before our Board, they brought blown-up posters that illustrated the large number of students enrolled in their programs.

"As you know, commissioners," an LGBT leader would explain, "the more students you have enrolled in your classes, the higher your Full Time Equivalency (FTE) and the greater your funding allocation from the state."

"We want to partner with you, to see you grow your enrolment and your state funding," was their pitch that made Board members nod their heads.

I was impressed. They were not on their knees begging for hand-outs. They were pushing for a "win-win" approach. They win, we win.

I was envious. This was how we should also have presented our case to the Board.

In the end, both Philippine Studies and LGBT Studies each got one of the 7 full time slots. We got ours because I was on the Board and part of the wheeling and dealing that takes place regularly in all the institutions that make political decisions affecting all of us. I was on the Board because the Filipino community worked for my election to a post I served in for 18 years.

We thereafter hired Dr. Leo Paz for that full time position and he grew the Philippine Studies program at City College until he retired last year.

That's what "political empowerment" means.

Ooooo

9
Remembering the First Quarter Storm
Jun 2015

To my father and his generation, the Japanese occupation of the Philippines was their most traumatic collective experience. To my generation, it was the declaration of martial law by the Dictator Ferdinand Marcos. While I was no longer in the Philippines by the time Marcos arrested and incarcerated thousands of my generation's best and brightest activists, I was there for the First Quarter Storm which occurred in the first three months of 1970 and which was the cathartic prelude to the imposition of martial law.

This week marks the 45th anniversary of that Storm.

Ferdinand Marcos had just been reelected president in November 1969 and was set to deliver the State of the Nation Address before a joint session of Congress.

Various student organizations jointly planned a protest rally, led by the National Union of Students of the Philippines (NUSP) headed by Edgar "Edjop" Jopson. I was part of the organizing committee as president of the National Union of High School Students (NUHS) which was aligned with the NUSP.

The rally brought together radicals and moderates who were united by our common opposition to the corruption of Ferdinand Marcos and his increasing militarization of the country.

Jopson was the featured rally speaker. After he spoke, Edjop called on Gary Olivar, a leader of the "radicals" A neighbor and one of my closest childhood friends, Gary was just about to speak when Edjop changed his mind and handed over the mike to radio commentator Roger "Bomba" Arrienda.

As Roger was delivering his speech laced with his usual bombast, the crowd kept yelling "Gary! Gary! Gary!" Instead of turning the mike over to Gary as we had agreed when we prepared the "united front" program of speakers, Edjop decided to end the rally by singing the national anthem. But just as the long rally was about to end at 6 p.m., a young labor leader grabbed the mike from Edjop and started delivering a fiery speech in Tagalog.

"Passions were high, exacerbated by the quarrel over the mike" wrote Jose F. Lacaba in his book, *Days of Disquiet, Nights of Rage,* "and the President had the bad luck of coming out of Congress at this particular instant."

Marcos was about to board his presidential limousine when someone hurled a crocodile papier mache in his direction. It missed him but it ignited a fury of retaliation by a phalanx of riot police who swung their rattan truncheons at the heads of students - moderates and radicals alike - unifying them in their common pain, as a stunned nation watched transfixed on live TV.

In the days that followed, indignation rallies denouncing police brutality were held in many campuses throughout Metro Manila culminating in the January 30 March to Malacanang from Plaza Miranda through the Mendiola Bridge. By nightfall, thousands of students surrounded the heavily fortified palace when suddenly the lights went off.

The Metrocom riot police retreated into the night, replaced with battle-hardened army soldiers armed with high-powered armalites out to quell a rebellion.

Before that long, dark bloody night was over, four students lay dead, scores paralyzed, and hundreds maimed from gunshot wounds.

As my high school classmate, Mario Taguiwalo, recalled: "The death of friends, the terror of gunfire, the taste of truncheon taught a lot of "isms" in one night. By the morning of January 31, 1970, a thousand chapters of student organizations had begun taking root in schools and communities nationwide."

The next three months were filled with protest demonstrations, rallies, and "people's marches" that all came to be called The First Quarter Storm, which another close friend, Nelson Navarro, described as "that cathartic student revolt in the first months of 1970 that shook the nation with its intense and all-encompassing life-changing experience."

I was a member of the secretariat of the Movement for a Democratic Philippines (MDP) that was formed to coordinate the demonstrations and rallies in 1970. A year later, my parents "exiled" me to San Francisco, fearful that I would share the same "salvaged" fate of so many student activists, like my friend, Charlie Del Rosario.

When Marcos declared martial law in September of 1972, he imprisoned thousands of activists, including many of my friends like Gary, Edjop, Mario and Jerry Barican, among the best and brightest of my generation.

Living through the martial law years in the United States, I taught Philippine history and political science at San Francisco State University and at Laney College. I went to law school, passed the bar, set up my private law practice, was appointed president of the San Francisco Public Utilities Commission, and was elected to the San Francisco Community College Board, the first Filipino elected to public office in San Francisco.

Twenty five years ago, on January 30, 1990, four years after People Power ended martial rule, I returned to Manila to attend a reunion I had organized, a gathering of friends at

Freedom Park in Malacanang Palace, to mark the 20th anniversary of the First Quarter Storm.

No longer present was my friend, Edjop, who became a revered people's hero after he was beaten, tortured, jailed for his underground anti-dictatorship efforts, and later executed by the military on September 20, 1982 when he was barely 34 years old.

But Jerry Barican was there. Once the radical president of the UP Student Council, he had become a staunchly conservative lawyer who justified his sea change by paraphrasing Churchill, "If you're not a radical by 18, you have no heart. If you're still a radical by 30, you have no head." Jerry went on to become a spokesman for President Joseph "Erap" Estrada.

Mario Taguiwalo was there too, proudly serving as President Cory Aquino's Undersecretary of Health. "Every time I am tempted to give up on people," Mario said, "I am reminded of the power of ideals deeply held and I persevere again seeking to convince and not to compel." Also there, among other friends, were Digoy Fernandez, a radical from De La Salle who had become a banker and Maan Hontiveros, an activist who was now the owner of her own communications company and her own low-cost airline.

Gary Olivar couldn't make it because he was busy in New York, working as a Sumitomo Bank executive after obtaining an MBA from Harvard University. But he sent me his message, which I read at the ceremony, about how "a singular dream moved a generation."

"A dream so compelling in its inception, so irresistible in its sweep, that it hurled thousands of us against the walls of this palace as if somehow through the sheer weight of our passions on that endless night, we would reclaim the palace for our own."

"In the conceit of our youth, we believed we could repair the broken bones of a people long despoiled and fulfill a dream of human freedom, of national sovereignty, of equitable progress for every Filipino."

Gary Olivar, the bright, articulate firebrand student leader who inadvertently caused the First Quarter Storm because he wasn't allowed to speak, became the official spokesman of President Gloria Macapagal-Arroyo.

"Reunions are beautiful," Nelson mused at the gathering, "because the older we get, the more we cease seeing ourselves as friends or enemies. We are simply survivors sharing a common memory."

Ooooo

10

Global Networking: Vision and Action for the Filipino Diaspora

(Speech delivered at the opening plenary session of the 3rd Global Summit of Filipinos in

the Diaspora held at the Manila Hotel, February 25-27, 2015).

The theme of this year âs Summit, "Vision and Action for the Filipino Diaspora 2015 and Beyond", has the stated goal of "providing a venue for continued networking and convergence of the Filipino diaspora councils" in order to "craft a common vision and development action plan for the Filipino Diaspora communities for 2015 and beyond".

We have convened our global Filipino Diaspora summits almost every other year since 2002 when we first came together at the Moscone Convention Center in San Francisco. Since then, we have met in Cebu, Honolulu, Sydney, Rome, and, for the last five years, here in Manila. When we started, there were representatives from only a few countries. Today the 600 registered delegates gathered here represent more than 30 participating countries.

We are set to meet again in 2017 but the venue is not certain. Our last three global summits have been held in Manila sponsored by the Commission on Filipinos Overseas (CFO) under the inspired leadership of Secretary Imelda Nicolas who believes as we do that Filipinos abroad should be seen "not just as a remittance sender but more of an active participant in the Philippines socio-economic-political development". Unfortunately, her CFO term coincides with that of Pres. Aquino whose presidency ends on June 30, 2016.

Thank you, Sec. Mely Nicolas and your CFO staff, for all your work to empower the Filipino Diaspora.

NOT OUR FINAL GLOBAL SUMMIT

A new president will be inducted into office on July 1, 2016 and he or she will then appoint a new head of the CFO. If the new president and the new CFO Secretary are opposed or indifferent to continuing support for the Filipino Diaspora, then this may be our last CFO-sponsored global summit. But it will not be the end of our biennial global summit of Filipinos. We will meet again in 2017 only perhaps not in Manila.

As we confront the prospect of where we will meet two years from now, let us look back at the Filipino Diaspora and reflect on where we have been and why we need to continue to empower ourselves as a global Filipino diaspora movement.

Diaspora is generally used to describe historic mass dispersions of people with common roots. It has also been defined as a transnational community of people with a shared identity as a singular ethnic group created by a forced or induced historical emigration from an original homeland.

Prof. Jonathan Y. Okamura from the University of Hawaii views the global Filipino Diaspora as an imagined community where

Filipinos, wherever they may be in the world, are aware of one another's presence and of the bonds of culture, national identity, custom and tradition that they share.

HISTORY OF THE FILIPINO DIASPORA

When Spain began its colonization of the Philippine Islands in 1565, it conscripted native Filipinos (Indios) to build Manila Galleon ships that would ply the trade route from Manila to Acapulco and to also serve as sailors on those ships. Once in Acapulco, many of the Filipino mariners chose not to return to Manila but instead to work on other ships that traveled to Spain and other ports in Europe.

In an 1892 editorial in La Solidaridad published in Barcelona, Spain, Editor Graciano Lopez Jaena noted the large presence of Filipino mariner communities in cities throughout Europe and as well as in Philadelphia, New York and New Orleans in the U.S.

Filipinos who jumped ship in New Orleans set up Filipino settlements in the marshlands of Barataria Bay, Louisiana â pioneering the dried-shrimp industry in the US - that became the subject of Lafcadio Hearn's 1883 article published in Harper's Weekly entitled "The Mahogany-Colored Manilamen of Louisiana."

After the Philippines was annexed by the U.S. in 1901, starting from 1906 through 1925, more than 125,000 Filipino workers were brought to the U.S. by the Hawaiian Sugar Planters Association to work on the sugar cane fields of Hawaii and then brought to the mainland to work on other crops in the farm valleys of the U.S.

After WW II, and through the 50s and 60s, tens of thousands of Filipinos were recruited to work on US Navy ships as stewards. After the liberalization of US immigration laws in 1965, at least 50,000 Filipino professionals and petitioned relatives of immigrants annually migrated to the US.

Much later, after martial law was declared in the Philippines in 1972, Filipinos were encouraged to work abroad â especially in the Middle East â in order to remit their salaries back to the Philippines to prop up the fragile economy. A new term entered the Philippine vocabulary â first, Overseas Contract Workers (OCWs) and then later, Overseas Filipino Workers (OFWs).

$26.93 BILLION ANNUAL REMITTANCE

According to data released by the Bangko Sentral ng Pilipinas (BSP), personal remittances from overseas Filipinos in 2014 set an all-time high for the Philippines at $26.93 billion, breaking the previous record of $25.35 billion posted in 2013. December of 2014 set the record for the highest monthly OFW remittance at $2.6 billion.

Ricardo B. Ramos observed that âthe Philippines is probably the only country in the world that has institutionalized the deployment of its people to work overseas, from professionals and skilled workers to domestic help,â since 1995, sending more than one million Filipinos annually to work abroad.

Now with about 14 million Filipinos in the Diaspora, the concept of the Filipino nation has changed. The old view that it refers exclusively only to those living within its land area boundaries is now obsolete. As former Chief Justice Artemio

Panganiban noted, "interactive news websites, cable TV programs, social networks like Facebook and Twitter, cell phones, Skype, Magic Jack, e-mails, teleconferencing and other electronic wonders no longer require actual physical presence to acquire thorough knowledge of Philippine political life."

Yes, overseas Filipinos know what is going in the Philippines but do Filipinos in the Philippines know or care about what is going on in the Filipino Diaspora?

In a 2003 Supreme Court decision, Justice Antonio Carpio commented that overseas Filipinos "are modern-day heroes and saviors of the economy. Their blood, toil, tears and sweat have propped up the Philippine peso through all the recurring financial crises that have battered the nation."

NOT JUST REMITTANCE SENDERS

That appears to be all that Filipinos in the Philippines know about Filipinos in the Diaspora. We are âremittance sendersâ, âsaviors of the Philippine economyâ. But do they know or care that thousands of Filipino OFW women are routinely raped by their employers in the Middle East? Do they know that some Philippine diplomats, instead of protecting our OFWs, even prey on them and demand and extract sex in exchange for emergency housing and funds to return back to Manila?

Two months after Marcos was deposed by People Power in 1986, Pres. Cory Aquino invited anti-Marcos Filipinos in America to visit her in Malacanang to express her appreciation for what overseas Filipinos did to help restore democracy back to the Philippines.

In that meeting, she asked us what she could do for us. On behalf of our group, I told her that we only have two requests: her support for overseas Filipinos to have the right to vote in Philippine elections and her support for dual citizenship to allow overseas Filipinos who have become citizens of their host countries to reacquire or retain their Philippine citizenship.

I told Pres. Cory Aquino that suffrage for overseas Filipinos would allow us to have a voice in the good governance of the country, in the election of leaders whose decisions affect overseas Filipinos and their families in the Philippines. It will also compel Philippine politicians to consider the needs and sentiments of overseas Filipino voters.

SUFFRAGE FOR OVERSEAS FILIPINOS

Pres. Aquino told us she would study dual citizenship but she expressed enthusiastic support for suffrage for overseas Filipinos. A year later, in the 1987 Philippine Constitution, she included as Article V, Section 2 the provision that: "The Congress shall provide a system for securing the secrecy and sanctity of the ballot as well as a system for absentee voting by qualified Filipinos abroad."

But despite her support, it would take another 16 years before the Overseas Absentee Voting Act would pass the Philippine Congress and be signed into law by Pres. Gloria Macapagal-Arroyo on Feb. 13, 2003. Unfortunately, that bill contained a "poison pill" that required absentee voters to sign an affidavit of intent to return to the Philippines within three years or face penalties of up to a year in jail, a provision that effectively killed any enthusiasm for overseas voting. It would take another decade of intense lobbying before this insane and onerous provision would be removed in an amended overseas voting bill that was signed into law by Pres. Benigno S. Aquino III on May 27, 2013.

But the damage was done. Because of this provision, which showed contempt for the "bagong bayani" (new heroes), only 850,000 overseas Filipinos have registered to vote and only a small fraction of that have actually voted.

AN EMPOWERED FILIPINO DIASPORA

We had hoped that if at least 5 million overseas Filipinos registered and voted, we would represent a significant portion of the electorate and constitute a major good governance force in Philippine politics. But that has not happened. The only way we can reach that goal is if the Philippines provided for Internet voting for overseas Filipinos especially for the 500,000 Filipinos who work in cruise ships and maritime cargo vessels. Given how long it takes to get anything to pass the Philippine Congress, it is not likely Internet voting will be enacted in time for the 2016 elections.

That is our challenge: how to be a significant force in the 2016 presidential elections despite our low voting numbers. How do we leverage our almost $27 billion a year in remittances to the Philippines to influence Philippine voters to support candidates endorsed by and supportive of the interests of OFWs?

We should ask the candidates what they plan to do to safeguard and protect our OFWs. We should ask the presidential candidates if he or she intends to continue the CFOâs support for the Filipino Diaspora and our biennial summits.

THE INDIA DIASPORA MODEL

One day, if we work for it, the Philippine government will develop an enlightened view of the Filipino Diaspora just as the Indian government has of its Diaspora. In 2004 India established the Ministry of Overseas Indian Affairs (MOIA) to connect the Indian Diaspora community with its motherland viewing the 2 million Indians in the Diaspora not just as âremittance senders but as "an important 'bridge' to access knowledge, expertise, resources and markets for the development of the country of origin."

Rodel Rodis, shown rightmost, with delegates.

"The success of this bridge is often predicated upon two conditions: the ability of the Diaspora to develop and project a coherent, intrinsically motivated and progressive identity and the capacity of the home country to establish conditions and institutions for sustainable, symbiotic and mutually rewarding engagement. Home countries are now beginning to recognize the need to pursue and promote the dynamic of the Diaspora and development."

"India's engagement with its Diaspora is symbiotic, the strands of both sides of the relationship equally important to create a resilient and robust bond. To engage with the Diaspora in a sustainable and mutually rewarding manner across the economic, social and cultural space is at the heart of the policy of the Ministry."

One day, there will be genuine overseas Filipino representatives in the Philippine Congress. One day, the Filipino Diaspora will be seen by the Philippine government as an integral part of the Philippines and included in the programs of all the executive departments and not just of one governmental agency. One day, our Global Summit of Filipinos in the Diaspora will have delegates from more than 100 countries and it will be attended by the president, cabinet members, senators, representatives all wanting to know what they can do to serve our needs.

That day will come, sooner than we think.

ooooo

11
Binay's Aguinaldo
Dateline: 2014

Money received from benefactors during Christmas in the Philippines is called "aguinaldo", a term and practice imported from Mexico during the Spanish colonial period where it traditionally referred to the annual Christmas bonus given to employees. In the Philippines, it is generically used to describe monetary gifts given by all benefactors, including godparents and employers.

Like all other "presidentiables", Vice President Jojo Binay is also expecting aguinaldos from his wealthy financial supporters. But down the road, he is also counting on another kind of "aguinaldo" from no less than the Philippine Supreme Court. It is a special gift that will allow him to succeed President Aquino as the next president of the republic.

Binay has a at least a 4 year head start on all his rivals as he has been campaigning relentlessly for the presidency since his election as vice-president in May of 2010. He has built a formidable infrastructure all over the Philippines from Batanes to Jolo, making contact with every governor, mayor and barrio captain throughout the land. He has amassed a campaign war chest that will likely exceed the campaign funds of all his opponents combined. But yet, he is not the "shoo-in" candidate he thought he would be.

Binay is presently facing two privately-filed plunder cases for the overpricing of the New Makati City Parking Building (P2.33 billion pesos) and the Makati Science High School Building (P1.33 billion pesos). He is also under investigation for his alleged ownership of a 350-hectare "high-end hacienda" in Rosario, Batangas that has its own world-class maze patterned after the Pew Garden in London, with an air-conditioned piggery, a flower orchard and a cock farm.

The Ombudsman is reportedly investigating these charges as well as Binay's foreign bank accounts that were not declared in his Statements of Assets and Liabilities (SALN). His former Vice Mayor, Ernesto Mercado, in sworn testimony before the Senate Blue Ribbon subcommittee, produced records of 7 foreign accounts in Hong Kong banks, 3 of which were under the "care of" Eduviges Baloloy, Binay's long-time aide. Deposits in these 3 accounts reached a total of US$ 71,481,95 (1996) and HK$957,912.93 (1996 and 1998).

The Ombudsman will likely ask the assistance of the Anti-Money Laundering Council (AMLC) to scrutinize Baloloy's bank records and any transfers of funds to Binay. This tracing of funds was successfully used during the impeachment of former chief justice Renato Corona where the Ombudsman and the AMLC tracked Corona's multiple bank accounts and numerous transactions involving amounts of P500,000 and above.

JUSTICE TAKES FOREVER

Binay has claimed that, as vice-president, he can only be removed by impeachment, a long process that is unlikely to be completed by the time of the May 2016 presidential elections. Even criminal charges that may be filed against him by the Department of Justice or plunder charges by the Ombudsman will take years to resolve.

When Binay's wife, Dr. Elenita Binay, was mayor of Makati in 2001 (when Jojo Binay was termed out of office), criminal charges were filed against her in connection with the irregular procurement of hospital beds worth P36.43 million for the Ospital ng Makati. It has taken more than 13 years for the case to even be set for trial last November 30 but even that was postponed again after Dr. Binay's lawyers filed yet another motion to further delay the proceedings.

If or when criminal and plunder charges are filed against Vice President Binay, the cases will undoubtedly end up in the Philippine Supreme Court where Binay, a skilled and experienced lawyer, will count on the Court to dismiss all the charges against him on the basis its previous unanimous decision involving Col. Rodolfo Aguinaldo.

Col. Aguinaldo was one of the worst violators of human rights during the Marcos dictatorship although he was never criminally charged in court for any of his offenses.

After the fall of Marcos, Aguinaldo joined the Reform the Armed Forces Movement (RAM) renegade forces of Senator Juan Ponce Enrile and Senator Gringo Honasan and attempted to topple the government of President Cory Aquino in December of 1989.

AGUINALDO'S RENEGADE TROOPS

Prior to his involvement in the failed coup, Aguinaldo ran for governor of Cagayan province in January of 1988. In a New York Times article about his candidacy that was published just before the elections ("*Renegade Officer Seeks Philippine Governorship*" January 18, 1988), Aguinaldo described to the New York Times reporter what he would do to anyone who tries to disarm his 1,400 renegade troops:

"They just start trying to disarm my men and I hit their houses and I wipe them out. At a given signal, we chop off the heads of anybody who is foolish. We will send them straight to hell, from the grandfather to the grandson."

Needless to say, no one dared to disarm Aguinaldo's men and he was easily elected to a four-year term as governor.

Because of his active involvement in the December 1989 coup attempt, Cory Aquino's Secretary of Local Government Luis Santos issued an administrative order removing Aguinaldo from his post as Cagayan governor. Aguinaldo appealed the Santos order and, while the appeal was pending in court, ran for reelection in May of 1992 and easily won again. He then filed a motion to dismiss the administrative charges against him on the basis of his reelection.

On August 21, 1992 (the 9th anniversary of Ninoy Aquino's assassination), the Philippine Supreme Court decided unanimously en banc in favor of Aguinaldo. Writing for a unanimous court, Associate Justice Rodolfo Nocon invoked the dicta of the Supreme Court case of Lizares v. Hechanova:

"The Court should never remove a public officer for acts done prior to his present term of office. To do otherwise would be to deprive the people of their right to elect their officers. When a people have elected a man to office, it must be assumed that they did this with the knowledge of his life and

character, and that they disregarded or forgave his fault or misconduct, if he had been guilty of any. It is not for the Court, by reason of such fault or misconduct, to practically overrule the will of the people."

http://www.lawphil.net/judjuris/juri1992/aug1992/gr_94115_1992.html

"Clearly then," the Supreme Court decreed, "the rule is that a public official can not be removed for administrative misconduct committed during a prior term, since his re-election to office operates as a condonation of the officer's previous misconduct to the extent of cutting off the right to remove him therefor."

BINAY'S ADMINISTRATIVE MIS-CONDUCT

Most of the charges against Binay involve "administrative misconduct" during his term as Makati mayor where he allegedly awarded lucrative contracts to cronies who rewarded him with substantial kickbacks. His election as president in 2016 will act as a "condonation" by the voters of this "previous misconduct" immunizing him from being removed from office.

So even if Binay is charged with plunder, he will still run for president while his case is proceeding through the notoriously long Philippine judicial process. After he is elected president, Binay's lawyers will file a motion to dismiss all the charges against him on the basis of the Aguinaldo precedent.

The Aguinaldo precedent is an egregiously bad decision that encourages people charged with criminal offenses to run for office to absolve themselves of any criminal charges under the doctrine of condonation. It embeds into law the Philippine culture of impunity.

Ooooo

12
Pope Francis' View of God
Dateline: Dec. 2014

Filipinos preparing to welcome Pope Francis to the Philippines on January 15, 2015 would do well to be familiar with the Pontiff's recently enunciated views, especially those which have drawn the ire of religious conservatives.

Shortly after his election a year ago, Pope Francis was heavily criticized for refusing to "judge" gays.

"When I meet a gay person, I have to distinguish between their being gay and being part of a lobby," he said. "If they accept the Lord and have goodwill, who am I to judge them? They shouldn't be marginalized. The tendency [to homosexuality] is not the problem…they're our brothers," he added.

He expressed the same mercy and compassion for the poor as he did for gays. Pope Francis declared two months ago in a speech in Rome at the World Meeting of Popular

Movements that "caring for the poor does not make you a communist" voicing concern that "land, housing and work are increasingly unavailable to the majority of the world's population."

Responding to his critics who accuse him of espousing Marxist views, he said: "They don't understand that love for the poor is at the center of the Gospel. Demanding this isn't unusual, it's the social doctrine of the church."

In recent weeks, Pope Francis has also been criticized for declaring that the Big Bang Theory and Evolution are not incompatible with the teachings of the Catholic Church.

"When we read about creation in Genesis, we run the risk of imagining God was a magician, with a magic wand able to do everything. But that is not so," Pope Francis said in a speech before the Pontifical Academy of Sciences meeting in Rome. "He created human beings and let them develop according to the internal laws that he gave to each one so they would reach their fulfillment," he explained.

Pope Francis has emphasized that the theory of evolution is not at odds with Catholic doctrine. "Evolution in nature is not inconsistent with the notion of creation, because evolution requires the creation of beings that evolve," he said.

Christian Creationist leader Ken Ham condemned Pope Francis for having "compromised biblical authority in favor of man's ideas in the area of origins." Ham claimed that the Pope's comments show "a lack of understanding of who scripture claims God is — the all-powerful

Creator, who is capable of doing what is impossible to man."

The controversy over the views of Pope Francis recalls an article that appeared in USA Today ("*View of God can predict values, politics*", Cathy Lynn Grossman, September 12, 2006) which reported that those who believe in one God "don't all have the same image of the Almighty in mind."

The article reflected on the findings of a study conducted by sociologists from Baylor University's Institute for Studies of Religion, a Baptist school of higher learning in Waco, Texas, which reviewed and analyzed the results of a Gallup Poll survey of 1,721 Americans who were each asked 77 questions with 400 answer choices.

The Gallup survey results revealed four distinct views of God.

-About 31.4% believe in an Authoritarian God who is "angry at humanity's sins and who is engaged in every person's life and world affairs" and "ready to throw the thunderbolt of judgment down on the unfaithful or ungodly." This view forms the core conviction of the American Religious Right.

According to Grossman's report, believers in an Authoritarian God "want an active, Christian-values-based government with federal funding for faith-based social services and prayer in the schools. They're also the most inclined to say God favors the USA in world affairs (32.1% vs. 18.6% overall)."

-About 23% believe in a Benevolent God which is a forgiving God ("more like the father who embraces his repentant prodigal son in the Bible") and believe that caring for the sick and needy ranks highest on the list of what it means to be a good person. "God is in control of everything. He's grieved by the sin of the world, by any created person who doesn't follow him. But I see (a) God ... who loves us, who sees us for who we really are. We serve a God of the second, third, fourth and fifth chance," says Rev. Jeremy Johnston of the 5,000 member Southern Baptist Congregation in Kansas.

-About 16% believe in a Critical God who has his "judgmental eye" on the world, but who will not intervene, either to punish or to comfort. According to Baylor's Christopher Bader, "this group is more paradoxical, They hold very traditional beliefs, picturing God as the classic bearded old man on high. Yet they're less inclined to go to church or affiliate seriously with religious groups. They are less inclined to see God as active in the world. Their politics are definitely not liberal, but they're not quite conservative, either."

Grossman writes that "those who picture a critical God are significantly less likely to draw absolute moral lines on hot-button issues such as abortion, gay marriage or embryonic stem cell research."

-About 24.4% believe in a Distant God who is "no bearded old man in the sky raining down his opinions on us" (Bader). They see a cosmic force that launched the world, and then left it spinning on its own. Bader believes that this has strongest appeal for Catholics, mainline Protestants, Jews, among "moral relativists" - those least likely to say any moral choice is always wrong - and among those who don't attend church.

Pope Francis clearly believes in the God of the New Testament, a Benevolent God who cares for the sick and the needy, not in the Authoritarian "fire and brimstone" God of the Old Testament who is always "ready to throw the thunderbolt of judgment down on the unfaithful or ungodly."

But how do Filipinos view God?

University of the Philippines Chancellor Dr. Michael Tan postulated in an Inquirer column that a majority of Filipinos believe in a somewhat distant but intervening God, literally a "tatay" [father] in the stereotyped sense. Filipinos tend to believe that natural disasters and personal misfortunes are punishment from God for our sins. But, Tan writes, "we also tend to see our relationships with that God as negotiable. We bargain all the time, vowing to do several novenas or have ourselves nailed to the cross in Lent, on condition that a certain favor is granted."

It may even be more confusing than that. Filipino Catholics pray to a dysfunctional Holy Trinity, believing in an Authoritarian God the Father, in a Benevolent God the Son, and in a somewhat Critical or Distant God the Holy Spirit.

But while we Filipinos are divided on our views of God, we are united in our devotion to the Blessed Virgin Mary. The Philippines is a "Marian" country. [My four sisters share "Maria" as their first names, as do millions of other Filipino women.] More than any other Catholic country in the world, the Philippines has embraced Mother Mary and iconic images of her are present in all Catholic Churches in the Philippines.

The Marian tradition goes all the way back to the origins of Christianity in the Philippines. The first church erected in Manila, the Nuestra Señora de Guia (the Ermita Church), prominently featured a statue of the Blessed Virgin.

Over one hundred Philippine parishes honor the Immaculate Conception, over sixty are dedicated to Our Lady of the Holy Rosary, while others carry various titles like the Assumption, Our Lady of Carmel, Mother of Perpetual Help, Our Lady of Lourdes.

In our devotion to the Blessed Virgin Mary, Filipinos have a kindred spirit in Pope Francis. While studying in Germany in the 1980s, the future pope saw a painting in a church in Augsburg that depicted Mary in heaven surrounded by angels, standing on a crescent moon crushing the head of the serpent, Satan, while untying a large knot on a ribbon.

When he was appointed the Archbishop of Buenos Aires, he introduced and encouraged devotion to Our Lady, Undoer of Knots, a devotion that became "a religious craze" (as the British Guardian called it) all over Argentina and Brazil. The prayer he composed became instantly popular.

"Virgin Mary, Mother of fair love, Mother who never refuses to come to the aid of a child in need, Mother whose hands never cease to serve your beloved children because they are moved by the divine love and immense mercy that exists in your heart, cast your compassionate eyes upon me and see the snarl of knots that exist in my life. You know very well how desperate I am, my pain, and how I am bound by these knots. Mary,

Mother to whom God entrusted the undoing of the knots in the lives of His children, I entrust into your hands the ribbon of my life. No one, not even the Evil One himself, can take it away from your precious care. In your hands, there is no knot that cannot be undone. Powerful Mother, by your grace and intercessory power with your Son and my liberator, Jesus, take into your hands today this knot."

God knows that Filipinos are desperately tied up in a snarl of knots and pray to the Virgin Mary to help undo the knots.

Pope Francis has made it clear that Mother Mary is not to be worshiped as a God but should be venerated as the highest of God's creatures "owing to her personal holiness, her assent to become Christ's earthly mother, and her faithfulness up to and beyond the Crucifixion". She is the model Christian who lives in heaven whom the people can turn to her to pray for them and to offer them support in hard times.

Filipino Catholics are Marianistas and so is their Pope.

ooooo

13
12 Million Metro Manila Commuters Stuck in Gridlock Hell

Guest Editorial: A Philnews.com
Dateline: 2014

For much of the last month, my Facebook friends in Metro Manila have been posting comments lamenting their helplessness at being condemned to spend a great portion of what is left of their productive lives stuck in hours of traffic with no hope in sight. They now appreciate why Dan Brown described Manila in his book, Inferno, as "the gates of hell" specifically referring to its "six-hour traffic jams (and) suffocating pollution".

A typical day in Metro Manila traffic.

It may just feel like six hours to those stuck in gridlock hell. "These days travel time in the streets of Metro Manila can be three times longer than usual, and this is during sunny days. With a heavy downpour and flash floods, the nation's premier region becomes paralyzed" was how the Philippine Star described it.

The Japan International Cooperation Agency (JICA), a reputable think tank, estimates that Metro Manila's traffic jams are costing the Philippine economy P2.4 billion pesos ($57 million) a day in potential income, a figure that JICA warns could balloon to P6 billion ($142 M) a day by 2030.

JICA also reported that traffic congestion leads to increased fuel consumption and automobile emissions as vehicles are forced to operate less efficiently. "More vehicles on the road means increased greenhouse gas emissions which lead to increased health costs."

Greenhouse gas emissions, JICA warned, are expected to increase to 5.72 million tons a year in 2030, compared to 4.7 million tons a year in 2012. As climate scientists explain, the increase in greenhouse gas emissions affects the frequency and ferocity of the natural calamities that bedevil the Philippines.

Rappler writer Katerina Francisco explains that JICA's P2.4 billion a day figure "includes lost work hours, lost **BUSINESS OPPORTUNITIES** due to delays and missed deadlines and wasted fuel." She observes that these annual losses (P576 billion a year) are greater than the P400 billion infrastructure budget for 2014. LINK

When an alternative 10 hour day/4 day work week schedule (similar to the schedule of some RNs in the US) was proposed as a way to ameliorate traffic gridlock, Sen. J.V. Ejercito expressed his opposition to the idea because of its effect on family life. According to Neal Cruz ("Will the 4 day work week work?"), Sen. Ejercito said "the employee who has to hurry home to cook for the family would get there very late and the children would be starving by the time dinner is served. Eating a late dinner means staying up late and therefore waking up late the next morning and arriving late in schools and offices. And most of the children and adults would be too sleepy to learn and work efficiently."

What Sen. Ejercito does not understand is that is precisely what happening now with a 5 day work week. Commuters who don't have chauffeurs to drive them around like Sen. Ejercito spend up to three hours commuting to and from work. The 4 day work week plan at least offers them hope of spending one less day in gridlock hell, which is precious time parents can spend with their children.

Sen. Ejercito and other government officials should follow the lead of Sen. Grace Poe and actually spend a day riding public transportation to work to appreciate the hell that their constituents are going through every day.

They may then consider other alternatives to easing traffic congestion like staggering the work hours of employees so that some of them can report for work at 10 am, 11 am or 12 noon and work until 6 pm, 7 pm or 8 pm. With less traffic, they may likely arrive home at the same time that they otherwise would when their work hours end at 5 pm.

What has exacerbated Manila's traffic mess is the decision of the Department of Public Works to embark this year on the simultaneous construction of 15 major road projects which are all expected to be completed by 2016. This has transformed an already congested metropolis into a traffic nightmare.

Government representatives explain that the public works projects are intended to solve traffic congestion and help the Philippines achieve "inclusive growth".

But UP Prof. Jose Regin Regidor questioned just exactly how "inclusive" the road projects can be when they are focused only on commuters who **USE CARS** and buses. Prof. Regidor said the government should spend more on mass transit systems to decongest a bursting mega city.

An example of what could be done to improve public transportation is what Bangkok recently entered into with a Japanese consortium to build an urban transit system there for $405 million.

As the Inquirer.**NET REPORTED** on November 4, 2013, "under the deal, ordered by Bangkok Metro Public Co., the consortium will construct a new 23-kilometer (14-mile) rail line in the Thai capital, the daily said, adding the rail operation is set to start in 2016. The Japanese group will supply 63 train cars and build the power grid, signals and rail yards as well as 16 stations for the project. It will also provide maintenance services under a 10-year contract and about 20 technicians with operational expertise will be stationed in Bangkok, the report said." LINK

Bangkok started its Metro Rail Transit system in 2004 serving a total of 240,000 passengers daily with 18 operational stations along 20 kilometers (12 mi) of underground route. Not content with the present MRT system,

Bangkok entered into a new contract with a Japanese consortium to construct a new 23-kilometer rail line with 63 trains in 16 stations **COMPLETE** with power grid, signals and rail yards and a 10-year maintenance and service contract with 20 technicians with operational expertise all for $405 million.

Like Bangkok, Metro Manila also has a rapid transit rail system in place called the Metro Rail Transit or MRT-3 which consists of a single line that runs in the general direction along the north and south lanes of Edsa Avenue serving close to 560,000 passengers a day. It was constructed by a consortium of private companies led by Robert John Sobrepena of the Fil-Estate Management, Inc. under a Build-Lease-Transfer arrangement which placed all the risks on the private companies to build the MRT system. The total cost for the project was $675.5 Million with $195 million provided by private sector funds an the balance obtained from foreign loans.

Department of Transportation and Communications (DOTC) head Joseph Emilio Abaya

The MRT-3 was inaugurated in 1999 and operated by Metro Rail Transit Corporation (MRTC), the private consortium. In 2010, the state-owned Land Bank of the Philippines and the Development Bank of the Philippines purchased a majority interest in the MRTC by buying out the holders of the foreign loans. Out of 14 members of the MRTC Board, 9 seats belong to government representatives with only 5 seats **ASSIGNED** to the private sector.

This effectively meant that the new MRTC was working at the direction of the Department of Transportation and Communications (DOTC) headed by Joseph Emilio Abaya, the former termed-out, three-term congressman from Cavite who previously chaired the House Appropriations Committee. He reportedly **RECEIVED** the largest allocation of funds (P408-M) from the Disbursement Acceleration Program (DAP) administered by Department of Budget Management Secretary Butch Abad.

Instead of expanding the current MRT-3 system that is serving 560,000 passengers daily at full capacity, as Bangkok did, the DOTC has instead asked the Philippine Congress to approve a P54 Billion pesos ($1.285 Billion) allocation in the next fiscal budget for the DOTC to purchase the state-owned bonds of the MRTC purportedly so that it can bid out the contract for a new maintenance provider. This request was endorsed by Budget Secretary Abad.

This is utter nonsense. This P54 Billion budget allocation is a total waste of government resources. It is twice what Bangkok is paying a Japanese consortium to construct a 23 kilometer rail line with 63 cars and a 10 year maintenance contract. The government should use this allocation to construct two more MRT lines to alleviate the congestion of the roadways.

Sen. Chiz Escudero, the chair of the Senate Committee on Finance, announced that he does not accept Abaya's explanation that the DOTC needs the P54 B in order to bid out the maintenance provider for the MRT. "The DOTC can bid that out now without shelling out P54 billion of taxpayer's money," Escudero pointed out.

Escudero said that he wants the P54 Billion that the DOTC plans to use for the buyout of the MRT to be used instead for more essential services for the general public like the much needed infrastructure to ease traffic congestion and disaster preparedness **PROGRAMS**.

The DOTC can use less than half of that allocation to enter into a contract with the Japanese consortium that is constructing a new line in Bangkok with a 10 year maintenance contract already built in along with 63 train cars and 16 rail stations. If a new MRT line carrying 500,000 passengers riders could be constructed, this would mean that about 8,000 buses can be taken out of Edsa. That is what will relieve the gridlock hell that is costing the Philippine economy $57 million a day in lost labor and income opportunities.

This P54 B allocation requested by the DOTC to buy out the shares of the government corporations is a minefield for corruption and should be rejected. It will just be a boondoggle for corruption and will only bring Manila closer to the "gates of hell." *Published 10/30/2014*

Ooooo

14
Why do bad things happen to good people?
Dateline: 2014

There are very few young people or "millennials" regularly attending mass at our local San Francisco parish, which is composed mostly of older people of all ethnic groups. Michael Marquez was that rare young man who regularly attended mass along withhis parents, Ramon and Patricia. A graduate of the local parochial schoolattached to our parish, Michael was genuinely well-loved by his fellowparishioners as he represented the bright future of our parish.

But that was not to be. On Sunday evening, November 22, Michael hadpizza with his girlfriend and a group of friends in nearby West Portal, and then, afterdropping his girlfriend off at her residence, proceeded home to Henry Street in Duboce Park with two friends. As they were walking down the tree-lined street, a car stopped beside them and 5 men alighted, one with a gun, barking instructions.

As Michael's friend, Jairo Rivera, reported. "They told all of them to get down to your knees and empty your pockets. I guess Mike didn't comply as well as they wanted him to, so they felt they had the need to shoot him." Michael was shot in the torso as the men seized his smart phone, wallet and backpack.

As Michael laid on the ground in a pool of blood, his friends called 911 and an ambulance soon brought Michael to the San Francisco General Hospital where he died.

http://abc7news.com/news/group-robs-kills-young-man-over-smartphone-in sf/408647/

FOOD FOR THE HOMELESS AND THE BIBLE

His father, Ramon, later told me that when his son's killers open his backpack, they will have to think twice about the life they took. His backpack carried food, leftovers from the restaurant where he worked, food which he would regularly hand out to the homeless people he would meet during the day.

"They will also find a Bible in his backpack," Ramon told me as he wept for his son. I told Ramon that if Michael doesn't make it to Heaven, then none of us have a chance.

My youngest son, Eric, who attended classes with Michael and who knew him since they were kids, attended a candlelight community vigil at the street where he was shot. It was overflowing with people as was the mass for Michael held at our parish a few days later. Everyone wept for Michael, for our church, for our community and for our society.

Why, God, why did you take Michael? Why not take drug addicts, the low-life scum who prey on our community? Why take the rare saint among a sea of sinners?

These were the questions asked at Michael's wake but they are also the type of questions people ask whenever seemingly senseless tragedies occur. Are we simply the random victims of fate or are the tragedies planned and controlled by a higher power?

Thornton Wilder, the novelist-playwright known most for his plays, Our Town, and The Matchmaker (which later became "Hello Dolly"), wrote his second novel, The Bridge of San Luis Rey, in 1927 to address these issues.

The opening sentence of "Bridge" describes the pivotal event of the book: "On Friday noon, July the twentieth, 1714, the finest bridge in all Peru broke and precipitated five travelers into the gulf below."

LIVE AND DIE BY ACCIDENT OR PLAN?

A witness to the tragedy, Brother Juniper, a Franciscan monk from Italy who happened to be in Peru, reflected on what he saw: "Why did this happen to those five?' If there were any plan in the universe at all, if there were any pattern in a human life, surely it could be discovered mysteriously latent in those lives so suddenly cut off. Either we live by accident and die by accident, or we live by plan and die by plan."

Brother Juniper then set out to "inquire into the secret lives of those five persons, that moment falling through the air, and to [surmise] the reason of their taking off."

In the course of his investigation, Brother Juniper discovers that they had all completed a problematic situation in their lives and that they were now ready to transition to the next phase.

But this book was fiction and the author can always create events that conveniently fit into his premise that people die after completing one phase.

This is not what happens in real life. Michael Marquez was not in transition when his life was snuffed out.

Neither were the 2900 victims of the Twin Towers terrorist attack in 9/11, nor the 58 victims of the Ampatuan Massacre in November of 2009, nor the 6500 victims of Super typhoon Haiyan/Yolanda in November of 2013. They were not in transition.

Wilder himself may have abandoned his original premise when he wrote another novel, 40 years later, that set up an alternative explanation for suffering.

In The Eight Day, a good, decent man is falsely accused of murdering his neighbor. In the course of clearing himself from the accusation of the bad guys who sought to frame him, he loses everything. The book does not end with his vindication and the villains punished.

TAPESTRY EXPLANATION

"Instead," Rabbi Harold Kushner explains, "Wilder offers us the image of a beautiful tapestry. Looked at from the right side, it is an intricately woven work of art, drawing together threads of different lengths and colors to make an inspiring picture. But turn the tapestry over and you will see a hodgepodge of many threads, some short, some long, some smooth and some cut and knotted, going off in different directions."

This was Wilder's new explanation, as Kushner explains it: "God has a pattern into which all of our lives fit....some lives are twisted, knotted or cut short, while others extend to impressive lengths, not because one thread is more deserving than the other but because the pattern requires it."

While this "tapestry" explanation can be comforting for some, it is ultimately unsatisfactory. How can human pain be justified just because it somehow contributes to a work of art?

Wilder's contrasting ideas on the reasons for why people suffer center on the common view that God was/is the cause of the suffering of man. Rabbi Kushner asks us to reconsider thatpremise:

"Could it be that God does not cause the bad things that happen to us? Could it be that He doesn't decide which families shall give birth to a handicapped child, that he did not single out Ron to be crippled by a bullet or Helen by a degenerative disease, but rather that He stands ready to help them and us cope with our tragedies if we could only get beyond the feelings of guilt and anger that separate us from Him? Could it be that "How could God do this to me?" is really the wrong question to ask."

It's like asking: How could God allow Hitler and his Nazis to exterminate six million Jews during WWII? There is a calming peace of mind that comes with accepting the fact that God did not intend for bad things to happen to good people. Evil acts are are beyond His intention or control. All we can pray for is the strength to overcome our pain and suffering.

- - - - - - -

This week marks the 29thanniversary of the death of our first child, Mariel, who died of cardiomyopathy just before reaching her first birthday. My wife, Edna, and I found this prayer below, written by Jack Riemer, which we shared with all our friends then and which we now share with you and the parents of Michael Marquez:

We cannot pray to You, O God, to banish war, for You have filled the world with paths to peace, if only we would take them.

We cannot pray to You to end starvation, for there is food enough for all, if only we would share it.

We cannot merely pray for prejudice to cease, for we might see the good in all that lies before our eyes, if only we would use them.

We cannot merely pray "Root out despair" for the spark of hope already waits within the human heart, for us to fan it into flame.

We must not ask of You, O God, to take the task that You have given us. We cannot shirk, we cannot flee away, Avoiding obligation forever.

Therefore we pray, O God, for wisdom and will, for courage to do and to become, not only to look on with helpless yearning as though we had no strength.

For Your sake and ours, speedily and soon, let it be: that our land may be safe, that our lives may be blessed.

ooooo

15
A Sometimes Clueless President
October 1st, 2014

"Aquino didn't snub Filipinos in US—Palace" blared the Sunday September 28 headline of INQUIRER.NET REPORT on Pres. Aquino's response to complaints from Filipinos in the US about his failure to meet with the Filipino community during his five-day visit to the US. The fact that Pres. Aquino's communications people had to respond so defensively is already a reflection of the cluelessness of Pres. Aquino and his advisers in Malacanang.

To accuse Pres. Aquino of being "clueless" may be too harsh. Certainly, he has not been clueless in dealing with the threat of China where he has admirably stood up to the new Asian imperial power. But when it comes to dealing with overseas Filipinos in general and Filipinos in the US in particular, he has been somewhat of a clueless mess.

For example, in the four State of the Nation Addresses (SONA) he has delivered since his election in May of 2010, Pres. Aquino has failed to include any mention of overseas Filipinos, not even a one line shout out to express thanks to the 12 million overseas hard-working Filipinos for remitting $24 billion a year to help prop up the Philippine economy.

This is especially disappointing for me to admit because the US Pinoys for Good Governance (USPGG.org) was formed in Manila after Pres. Aquino was inaugurated as president on June 30, 2010 when 200 Filipinos from the US, who all campaigned for him, traveled to Manila to personally attend his inauguration. We then convened the First Worldwide Conference of Overseas Filipinos for Good Governance at the Sofitel Hotel on July 1-2, 2010.

In the four years since then, USPGG has supported the good governance initiatives of Pres. Aquino and in leading the global campaign to expose and oppose China's creeping invasion of the Philippines. In the US, the group has also been active in the Filipino American community's campaign to request the US Department of Homeland Security (DHS) to grant Temporary Protected Status (TPS) to the Philippines in response to the destruction caused by Super Typhoon Haiyan/Yolanda.

Temporary Protected Status (TPS)

TPS is the most important issue of concern to the community of four million Fil-Ams as it offers the opportunity to temporarily legalize the status of perhaps as many as 500,000 Filipinos who are out of status and living in constant fear of deportation, popularly known as TNTs (*takot na takot* – very fearful).

More than 200 Filipino community organizations in the US are actively engaged in supporting the grant of TPS to the Philippines – from the National Federation of Filipino American Associations (NaFFAA) to the National Alliance for Filipino Concerns (NAFCON), from the

Migrant Heritage Commission (MHC) to the National Domestic Worker Alliance (NDWA) and the Rescue2Recovery coalition. Fil-Am Republicans and Fil-Am Democrats have set aside their political differences to unite on this issue.

After more than 10 months of intensely lobbying the Obama Administration, the Fil-Am community reached the consensus that what was needed to get TPS granted was for Pres. Aquino to make a personal request to Pres. Obama.

Fil-Am community leaders then sought a personal meeting with Pres. Aquino at any time during his five-day visit to the US to inform him about TPS and about our request for him to talk to Pres. Obama. Loida Nicolas-Lewis, USP4GG national chair, wrote Philippine Ambassador to the US Jose Cuisia, Jr. requesting a community meeting with Pres. Aquino at any time during his US visit.

Amb. Cuisia is keenly aware of the Fil-Am community's concern about TPS. On August 15, he hosted a Fil-Am community leaders' meeting at the Philippine Embassy in Washington DC with top officials of the US Department of Homeland Security (DHS). At that meeting, DHS Assistant Secretary Alan Bersin informed the community that the DHS was in the final stage of deliberating on the issue of TPS for the Philippines.

http://globalnation.inquirer.net/109691/ why-tps-matters-even-now

Amb. Cuisia relayed our request for a meeting to Pres. Aquino. Regretfully, he informed us, Pres. Aquino's schedule did not allow for even a half hour meeting with him during his five-day US visit. But Amb. Cuisia said that Department of Foreign Affairs (DFA) Secretary Albert Del Rosario was willing to meet with Fil-Am community leaders in New York to discuss TPS.

Sec. Del Rosario met with Fil-Am community leaders on September 24 in a meeting where he assured the Fil-Am leaders of the full support of the Philippine Government in pushing the TPS request. "We stand with you on this issue," Secretary Del Rosario said.

What Pres. Aquino did in San Francisco

On the same day that Sec. Del Rosario was meeting in New York meeting with Fil-Am community leaders, Pres. Aquino arrived in San Francisco. It would just be a brief stopover on his way back to Manila, we were told, so there would be no opportunity for Pres. Aquino to meet with the San Francisco Fil-Am community.

But we were misinformed. Upon his arrival at the San Francisco International Airport, Pres. Aquino was escorted by a large convoy of San Francisco police cars and motorcycles to the San Francisco offices of Wells Fargo Bank Chairman John Stumpf and other bank officials. He later also met with Gary Loveman, CEO of Caesar's Entertainment Corporation; and Steven Tight, president of International Development.

In the INQUIRER "snub" report, Aquino's Communications Secretary Herminio Coloma said, "During the short period of time his plane was in San Francisco, the President met with leaders of two multinational companies on entertainment and banking who expressed interest in investing or expanding their current participation in the robust economy of our country."

"Short period of time?" Pres. Aquino did not return back to the airport to return to Manila after his meeting with the business leaders. Instead, he directed his police escorts to take him to San Francisco's fabled Haight-Ashbury district, not to tour the birthplace of the 1960's Hippie Revolution but to eat burgers at MacDonald's and to do some shopping for jazz CDs at Amoeba Music across the street. The Haight visit snarled traffic and caused residents to post Instagram

photos on Twitter showing the rows of SFPD motorcycles and cars parked along Haight mocking Aquino's message of climate change.

Why couldn't Pres. Aquino have stopped to eat at a Filipino restaurant to show support for local Fil-Am owned businesses? How can he ask Fil-Ams to support the Philippines when he can't even patronize Fil-Am businesses in the US?

From the Haight, Pres. Aquino then proceeded to the Peninsula Gun Store in San Bruno where he even had a photo taken with Jeff Downs, a gun store employee who posted a photo of Aquino and him on his Facebook page with the caption: "The president of the Philippines decided to stop by and buy some stuff. Really nice man!"

Downs said that Aquino was "interested in the EO tech optics for rifles. I guess it's really hard to get them in the Philippines so he was able to get them here. Some of his members of his entourage were able to pick up some stuff too... He spent a decent amount of money but I don't think it will be appropriate for me to say," Downs said.

http://www.balitangamerica.tv/preside
nt-aquino-stops-by-gun-store-before-flight-
back-to-ph/

Guns are an especially sensitive issue in America where gun massacres — like the Sandy Hook Elementary School Massacre in Connecticut in November of 2012 where 27 children killed — have become commonplace. Aquino's visit to a gun store may cause people to change the country's tourist slogan to "More Gun in the Philippines."

Clearly, Pres. Aquino had time to meet with the Fil-Am community but chose not to. Balitang America, the ABS-CBN daily news show on cable TV with 250,000 US subscribers, asked its viewers on September 24, "Should Pres. Aquino have taken the time to meet with the Fil-Am Community during his recent US trip?"

The following day the response of the viewers showed 71% yes and 29% no.

http://www.balitangamerica.tv/isyu-
results-sept-25-2014/

Pres. Aquino measured the success of his Europe trip by the $2.3 billion in investment pledges he said he received from businesses there. He would have received much more than that if he had supported TPS. We wanted the opportunity to explain the economics of TPS to him.

We would have told him that in the US, all employers are required to submit an I-9 form to the DHS attesting to the employment eligibility of their employees. Employers hiring "illegals" are fined $2,000 per employee and can be <u>JAILED</u> after two or more offenses. This law makes it difficult for Filipinos TNTs to find good-paying jobs as they are often at the mercy of employers who pay them low wages. If they complain, they could be deported. Despite working low wages and living in poor housing, the TNTs still manage to remit about $200 a month to their relatives in the Philippines.

If TPS is granted to the Philippines, then every TNT can be given temporary legal status, which means that employers can legally hire them and pay them the minimum wage ($9/hour in California, $10.50/hour in San Francisco). This means that TNTs can now remit at least $500 a month to the Philippines. If there are 300,000 Filipino TNTs, as the DHS believes, then that means that $150 million would be remitted to the Philippines every month or $2 billion per year. In two years, that would be twice the amount Aquino received in pledges from the European businesses who expressed interest in investing in the Philippines.

If TPS is not granted to the Philippines, then the Fil-Am community may blame Pres.

Aquino for not caring enough about Filipino TNTs to make a personal phone call to Pres. Obama. He was too busy checking out the latest gun optics for rifles to bother.

What could have been

Pres. Aquino should read about the "rapturous welcome" accorded to India Prime Minister Narendra Modi at the Madison Square Garden in New York while he was there to attend the United Nations Climate Change Summit.

Modi spoke before an audience of more than 18,000 Indians who chanted "Modi, Modi, Modi" as he told them of his plans to simplify the immigration bureaucracy for Indians living abroad, and as he called on them to "join hands to serve our mother India."

More than 30,000 Indians out of a US Indian population of 2.3 million had <u>APPLIED</u> for the 18,000 free tickets to cheer their prime minister. If Pres. Aquino had announced his enthusiastic support for TPS and reported on his personal call to Obama, the 20,000- seat capacity Staples Center in Los Angeles would have been filled to the rafters with Filipinos chanting "PNoy! PNoy! PNoy!"

There are likely more than 500,000 TNTs in the US and they alone would have filled the seats but Staples Center would also have been filled with thousands of Filipinos applauding his assertion of national sovereignty in the West Philippine Sea and his filing an action against China in the International Tribunal on the Law of the Seas (ITLOS).

But unlike Aquino, Modi and his predecessors greatly value the contribution of

Indians abroad. India has a cabinet-level Ministry of Indians Abroad (**moia.gov.in**) which proclaims in its website that "in this increasingly inter-dependent and inter-connected world, Overseas Indians are becoming 'Global Citizens'. Even so, our shared culture and shared values bond all of us together."

Pres. Aquino has a "myopic view" of overseas Filipinos. To get a clue about what this means, he should read the MOIA website:

"The emergence of significant Diasporas has in recent years brought into sharp focus two key facts. First, there is a large expatriate population of skilled people from emerging economies in the developed world. Second, overseas communities can constitute a significant resource for the development of the countries of origin. The movement of the high skilled and low skilled workers from less to more developed economies and back opens several new opportunities for development. **To view the Diaspora only through the looking glass of remittances and financial flows is to take a myopic view. Not all expatriates need to be investors and their development impact measured only in terms of financial contributions to the home country.**

"**An overseas community can and does serve as an important 'bridge' to access knowledge, expertise, resources and markets for the development of the country of origin. The success of this bridge is often predicated upon two conditions: the ability of the Diaspora to develop and project a coherent, intrinsically motivated and progressive** identity and the capacity of the home country to establish conditions and institutions for sustainable, symbiotic and mutually rewarding engagement. Home countries are now beginning to recognize the need to pursue and promote the dynamic of the Diaspora and development."

If he's not too busy playing with his imported EO optics for his rifle and listening to his jazz records, perhaps Pres. Aquino may have the time to read this article to get a clue about why Filipinos in the US are so disappointed in him.

ooooo

16
The Self-Perpetuating Elite of the Philippines
Undated

In the July 1968 issue of the American magazine *Foreign Affairs*, a novice Filipino senator introduced his country to the American people as "a land in which a few are spectacularly rich while the masses remain abjectly poor. . . . a land consecrated to democracy but run by an entrenched plutocracy… a people whose ambitions run high, but whose fulfillment is low and mainly restricted to the self-perpetuating elite…a land of privilege and rank – a republic dedicated to equality but mired in an archaic system of caste."

The young senator should have also shared his insights with the Filipino people ashis thoughtful   essay should also have   been published in the Philippines and should have been required reading in Philippine schools. It still should be, even now - 46 years later.

The young author was Sen. Benigno "Ninoy" Aquino, Jr., a member of the "entrenched plutocracy" and the "self-perpetuating elite" of the Philippines.

Ninoy Aquino came from a "prosperous family of hacenderos" (Wikipedia), a family which gained prominence when his grandfather, Servillano Aquino, served as a general in Pres. Emilio Aguinaldo's Revolutionary Army. Aquino's father Benigno Aquino, Sr. was elected to the Philippine House of Representatives in 1919 before winning a Philippine Senate seat in 1928, the first of many Aquinos to be elected to the Senate including Ninoy, his son Noynoy, his siblings Butz and Tess, and his nephew Bam.

While Aquino was the youngest Filipino politician ever to be elected mayor (at age 22), governor (at age 29) and senator (at age 34), he never got to be the country's youngest president because Marcos declared martial law in 1972 voiding the 1973 presidential elections where Aquino was favored to win. While Aquino never became president because of his assassination in 1983, his widow, Cory, and his son, Noynoy, were both elected to the country's top post.

ORIGIN OF THE S.P.E.

The origin of the "self-perpetuating elite" of the Philippines can be traced to the decision of the Spanish colonizers in the third century of their rule to appoint the mostprominent local Ilustrados in each town and province as gobernadorcillos to collect taxes from the people.

When the Americans colonized the Philippines at the turn of the 20th century, they continued the Spanish colonial practice and appointed local Ilustrados to political positions as well.

Uncomplicated Mind blogger Joe Rivera wrote: "When the U.S. colonized the Philippines at the turn of the 20th century, they took these Ilustrados under their wings and trained them for the practical affairs of popular government. The first American civil governor of the islands, William Howard Taft, believed that the rudiments of self-government would easily be transferable to these Ilustrados, the oligarchic elite, because of their social and economic status. So, it was the fault of the American colonizers that spawned the political dynasties we have now."

In every province of the Philippines, political power was wielded by the local Ilustrados who kept political power limited to their families making the surnames Osmena, Lopez, Cojuangco, Roxas, Aquino, Macapagal and Marcos household names in Philippine politics.

Rivera described the consequence of Taft's Ilustrado policy: "Taft's idea of letting society's affluent members constitute the Philippine Assembly in 1907 and Congress in the ensuing years resulted in the formation and circulation of elites that perpetuate their hold on political offices. A truly representative democracy failed to flourish, shattering the hopes that the country would now be able to draw upon all classes in Philippine society in electing public officials."

As Carlos Conde noted in his New York Times article, *Family dynasties bind politics in the Philippines*, (May 11, 2007), "political dynasties were an offshoot of the country's colonial experience, in which the Filipino elite was nurtured by Spanish and American colonizers. Even after the country gained independence, in 1946, the largely feudal system persisted, as landed Filipino families sought to protect their interests by occupying public offices."

Conde added: "There are an estimated 250 political families nationwide, with at least one in every province, occupying positions in all levels of the bureaucracy... Of the 265 members of Congress, 160 belong to these clans."

According to one estimate, 40 percent of provincial congressmen and governors are related, and 50 percent of both are related to previous holders of those offices.

"These are the same families who belong to the country's economic elite, some of them acting as rule makers or patrons of politicians who conspire together to amass greater economic power," said Roberto Tuazon, director of the Center for People Empowerment in Governance.

NON-ILUSTRADO ELITE

But even when a political figure with no ties to the traditional Ilustrado elite emerges, he quickly develops the impulse to amass and perpetuate political power in his family.

An example is Joseph Ejercito who was born to an upper middle class family in Tondo, Manila, and who became a popular movie actor under his screen name,"Joseph Estrada", after he was expelled from Ateneo University. He parlayed his fame as an actor to be elected mayor of San Juan, a post from which he then ran for and was elected variously as senator, vice-president and then as president in 1998.

After Estrada was removed from office in 2001 by "People Power II", his first wife, Dr. Loi Ejercito, was elected to the senate, followed by one son, Jinggoy, and yet another son, J.V. Ejercito. His nephew, ER Ejercito (real name George Estregan, Jr.) was elected Laguna governor in 2010 (although he may soon be removed from office for "overspending"). Even after a plunder conviction and a sentence of life imprisonment, "Erap" Estrada managed somehow to be elected mayor of Manila in 2013.

Like Estrada, the man widely assumed to be the next president of the Philippines, Vice-President Jejomar "Jojo" Binay, also did not descend from the Ilustrado elite. Orphaned at nine years old, Binay was adopted by his uncle, Ponciano, a man of modest means. Binay studied at regular local schools before acquiring a law degree from the University of the Philippines. As a lawyer, Binay volunteered to provide free legal assistance to victims of human rights abuses during the Marcos dictatorship.

Because he was an ardent supporter of Cory Aquino in the 1986 People Power Uprising, Binay (later known as "Rambotito") was rewarded with an appointment as mayor of Makati in 1986. He was elected in his own right in 1988, then reelected in 1992 and 1995 when term limits required him to relinquish the post to his wife, Elenita Binay, who was elected mayor in 1995. Binay was elected mayor again 1998 and again until 2010 when he ran and won as Vice-President.

FILIPINOS VOTE FOR FAMILY, NOT CLASS OR IDEOLOGY

Since Binay's mayoral appointment in 1986, Makati has known no other mayor not named Binay. After he was elected VP in 2010, his son, Jejomar Erwin "JunJun" Binay, Jr., succeeded him as mayor. One daughter, Mar-Len "Abigail" Binay is a House member representing Makati while another daughter, Nancy, was elected to the Senate in 2013 despite having absolutely no prior job experience other than as her father's "executive assistant".

Conde observed that members of dynasties, like the emerging Binay Dynasty of Makati, have "developed a sense of entitlement regarding public positions" as evidenced by Makati Mayor JunJun Binay order to arrest three Dasmarinas Village security guards who were not aware that the mayor of Makati is exempt from complying with rules for ordinary citizens not allowed to pass through certain gates past a certain hour. What is unfortunate is that "many ordinary Filipinos accept the (entitlement) arrangement as inevitable, which makes it difficult to change the situation."

https://www.youtube.com/watch?v=ojF Go9RN5mY

In his widely-read 1988 essay, A Damaged Culture, James Fallows wrote: "when observing Filipino friendships I thought often of the Mafia families portrayed in The Godfather: total devotion to those within the circle, total war on those outside. Because the boundaries of decedent treatment are limited to the family or tribe, they exclude at least 90 percent of the people in the country."

Anthropologist Brian Fegan asserts in his book, "*An Anarchy of Families: State and Family in the Philippines*", that Filipinos tend not to vote according to class, ethnicity, religion or even ideology. They vote for family which has become "the most enduring political unit and the one into which, failing some wider principle of participation, all other units dissolve."

The system of family clan dominance is a vicious cycle, Political Science Prof. Julio Teehankee asserts, because it "prevents the expansion of the base of aspirants and candidates for representation." The result, he added, is a political system dominated by patronage, corruption, violence, and fraud.

CLAN DOMINANCE

The dominance of the family clans has prevented the flowering of democracy in the Philippines.

"Continuing clan dominance is a product of the seemingly immutable and unequal socioeconomic structure, as well as the failure to develop a truly democratic electoral and party system," said Prof. Teehankee (quoted by Conde).

The system is a vicious cycle, one that prevents the expansion of the base of aspirants and candidates for representation, Teehankee said. The result, he added, is a political system dominated by patronage, corruption, violence, and fraud.

This is the political system that has produced fixers like Janet Lim Napoles who conspired with the dynasts in Congress to steal taxpayer money intended to provide the people with much needed services and infrastructure improvements.

Among the senators disclosed by Napoles as having received billions of pesos of kickbacks from her pork barrel scams are past and present senators including: Juan Ponce-Enrile, Jinggoy Estrada, Bong Revilla, Gringo Honasan, Loren Legarda, Loi Ejercito, Vic Sotto, Rodolfo Biazon, Tessie Aquino-Oreta, Ferdinand "Bongbong" Marcos, Jr., Manny Villar, Chiz Escudero, Cynthia Villar, Aquilino "Koko" Pimentel, Jr., Aquilino "Nene" Pimentel Sr., Alan Peter Cayetano and Lito Lapid.

Not all the "self-perpetuating elite" of the Philippines conspired with Napoles but all those who did were certified members of the "self-perpetuating elite".

Ooooo

17

Are Filipinos United Against China's Invasion of Ayungin Shoal?

A Philnews.com Guest Editorial, 2013

At a fund raiser for the Filipino Advocates for Justice in Oakland on June 20, I sat down with the former national chair of Bayan USA to ask him if his group planned to join the July 24 global protest against China's occupation of the Ayungin Reef.

I told him that two years ago, when the US Pinoys for Good Governance (USP4GG) was planning protest demonstrations in front of all the Chinese consulates in the US, his friend, Raquel Redondiez, the national chair of Gabriela USA and former Secretary-General of Bayan USA, told Balitang America reporter Henni Espinosa that her group was resolutely opposed to Filipino global protest actions against China because, she said, "it will only worsen the conflict between China and the Philippines."

Raquel told Henni in the TV interview that was aired on Balitang America on May 9, 2012, that "when there is a conflict between siblings or friends, you usually want to start talking one-on-one before you bring in other people or mediators."

"China is not the true bully in this standoff," Raquel insisted. "The China threat is being used by the U.S. to actually further trample on our national sovereignty."

But three Chinese naval ships from Sansha have surrounded Ayungin Reef since May 8 and Major Gen. Zhang Zhaozhong of the People's Liberation Army (PLA) has openly announced on Beijing TV China's plans to set up a blockade to prevent the Philippine marines stationed at Ayungin Reef from receiving fresh supplies.

"Only a few troopers are able to station there," he said, "but there is no food or even drinking water there. If we carry out the cabbage strategy, they will not be able to send food and drinking water onto the islands. Without the supply for one or two weeks, the troopers stationed there will leave the islands on their own. Once they have left, they will never be able to come back."

Is this conflict with China really one "between siblings and friends" as Redondiez claims? Seriously?

I explained that the July 24 global protest date is significant because it marks the first anniversary of Beijing's establishment of the Sansha prefecture to supervise 2 million square kilometers of the South China Sea including the West Philippine Sea and the Kalayaan Island Group which lie within the 200 mile Exclusive Economic Zone (EEZ) of the Philippines according to the United Nations Convention on the Law of the Seas (UNCLOS).

"Are you anti-imperialist?" I asked him.

"Of course!" he replied.

"Well then," I asked, "what is the essential difference between what the US did to the Philippines in 1899, what Japan did to the Philippines in 1942 and what China is doing to the Philippines now? Are you just anti US imperialist but not anti-Chinese imperialist?"

Ayungin Reef is the gateway to the Recto Bank, I explained, and Recto Bank, which is only 85 nautical miles from Palawan, may contain as much as 213 billion barrels of oil and 2 quadrillion cubic feet of natural gas, according to the US Energy Information Agency (EIA). The future of the Philippines is in Recto Bank: "Our soil, our oil."

"If China completes its illegal occupation of Ayungin Reef, it will only be a matter of time before China proceeds to occupy Recto Bank," I said. "But," he protested, "only the rich ruling class of the Philippines will benefit from the exploitation of Recto Bank's resources."

"That's true, now," I answered. "But don't you guys want to overthrow that ruling class so that the Philippines is governed by workers and peasants? If you allow China to seize all the oil and natural gas of the Philippines now, what will be left for the Filipino workers and peasants to use in the future? Do you expect China to just return all of our oil and natural gas when the People's Republic of the Philippines is proclaimed?"

If that was his naïve belief, I would have told him about what happened on March 14, 1988 to the brave sailors of the People's Republic of Vietnam who refused to take down their flag and leave the Johnson South Reef that is within the EEZ of Vietnam which China is claiming it owns. China's four warships then pounded the reef with 37 mm anti-aircraft artillery directly shooting and killing 64 unarmed or lightly armed Vietnamese sailors. China filmed its slaughter of the Vietnamese sailors and aired the footage all over China to show that China means business.

What happened to the Vietnamese Navy sailors in 1988 may happen to the Philippine Navy sailors. On June 21, 2013, the Reuters news agency reported from Beijing that China condemned the Philippines' "illegal occupation" of the Ayungin Reef after the Philippines moved new soldiers and supplies to the BRP Sierra Madre, a sunken WW II vessel which has served as the Philippines' marine outpost in the Ayungin Reef since 1999.

"China's determination to safeguard its national sovereignty is resolute and unwavering and (we) will never accept any form of illegal occupation of the Ren'ai Reef (Ayungin Reef) by the Philippines," Chinese Foreign Ministry spokeswoman Hua Chunying told reporters in a briefing in Beijing.

Ayungin Reef is just 105 miles from Palawan and almost 600 miles from the nearest China port and yet China claims the Philippines is illegally occupying Chinese property? What brazen gall!

This is the time for Filipinos all over the world to rally to the flag of the Philippines. But, unfortunately, there are organizations like Bayan and Gabriela USA which are advancing the political line that our dispute with China is just between "siblings and friends."

The website of Bayan USA (bayanusa.org) shows that, along with Gabriela USA, they have a have a large number of affiliates all over the US like Anakbayan and the Committee for Human Rights in the Philippines. Proof of their clout and influence is the impressive showing of their partylist groups, Gabriela and Bayan Muna, in the May 13 Philippine elections.

Though the words may sound alike, Bayan and Anakbayan should not be confused with Akbayan. In the Philippine political spectrum, the former groups are viewed as the far left while the latter is considered the "democratic left". They have fundamental differences on a mountain of issues including China.

Akbayan has been firmly opposed to China's "creeping invasion" of the Philippines and its members have been actively involved in organizing and participating in all the local protest rallies against China. Akbayan's national chair, Rissa Hontiveros, was the spokesperson of the coalition that organized the anti-China rally on July 8, 2011. Its partylist representative, Rep. Walden Bello, led a House delegation to the Kalayaan Island Group in 2011, a move which was heavily criticized by Beijing.

Recently, on June 11, 2013, Rep. Bello led a "fish protest" in front of the China Consulate in Makati to "express outrage against the atrocious poaching activities in the West Philippine Sea by the Chinese government. China aims to stake a monopoly over the fishing and energy resources of the West Philippine Sea in its bid to become a regional hegemon. This is at the expense of destroying the marine ecosystems in the area and subverting its neighbors' sovereignty," Rep. Bello said.

On the other hand, the Bayan and Anakbayan organizations and their affiliates take their cue on the China issue from Jose Maria Sison, the founding chairman of the Communist Party of the Philippines. In a statement issued on April 30, 2012, Sison wrote: "China has shown a preference for economic and diplomatic action rather than military action in international affairs..... What the US is bent on doing is to manage and manipulate the Philippine-China contradictions in order to further entrench itself militarily in the Philippines, continue to violate our national sovereignty and territorial integrity, serve as the bantay salakay, and intensify its efforts to strengthen US hegemony over the Asia- Pacific region."

Those interested in protesting US imperialism can join Bayan and Anakbayan members and their affiliates in their almost daily demonstrations in front of the US Embassy on Roxas Boulevard.

Those interested in protesting China's imperialism are invited to attend a major protest rally in front of the China Consulate in Makati on Wednesday, July 24 at 12 noon. On that day in New York, Filipinos from all over the East Coast will converge at the United Nations to protest China's occupation of the Ayungin Reef and to draw attention to the arbitral petition of the Philippine government before the UN International Tribunal on the Law of the Sea.

There will also be simultaneous demonstrations in front of all the China consulates in the US and all over the world. "We want to serve notice on China that its Sansha garrison navy has no jurisdiction over the Philippines," USP4GG spokesman Ted Laguatan said.

"Stop China's Invasion of the Philippines!" *Published 7/2/2013*

Ooooo

18

Telltale Signs: "Why are there so many Filipino nurses in the US?"

Dateline, 2013

This was the question posed to me by a curious TV reporter on May 7, just three days after a stretch limousine hired to carry nine Filipino nurses to a bridal party across the San Mateo Bridge suddenly burst into flames killing five of the occupants, including the bride.

When she interviewed me in my law office in San Francisco, Ann Notarangelo, the weekend anchor of CBS 5's Eyewitness News, explained that she was only asking the question because it was on the minds of her viewers. She thought I might know the answer as I taught Filipino American History at San Francisco State University and I am the legal counsel of the

Philippine Nurses Association of Northern California. Plus, I told her, I am married to a Filipino nurse.

Ann said that she was frankly surprised to learn that one out of every five registered nurses in California is a Filipino, a considerably large percentage since Filipinos number only 2.3 million (officially 1.2 million) out of a state population of 38 million.

"I never noticed it before," Ann observed, "because I generally don't see people in racial terms." But, she said, in reflecting back on all the times she visited friends and relatives in hospitals all over the California, she now recalls seeing Filipino nurses everywhere. And, I added, not just in California.

NO LONGER INVISIBLE

The seeming anonymity of Filipino nurses in the US - of being there but not being quite there - is likely no more. The video clip of the fire-engulfed limousine taken by a passing motorist using a cell phone was the top story in the US over the weekend. Americans learned that the fatalities included Neriza Fojas, 31, a newlywed bride who was planning to get married again in the Philippines in June; Michelle Estrera, 35, the bride's Maid of Honor who worked with her at a Fresno medical facility; Jennifer Balon, 39, and Anna Alcantara, 46, of San Lorenzo, who both worked at the Fruitvale Healthcare Center; and Felomina Geronga, 43, who worked at the Kaiser Permanente Medical Center in Oakland.

Americans also learned about the nurses who escaped the fire and were treated for burns and smoke inhalation: Mary G. Guardiano, 42;

Jasmine Desguia, 34; Nelia Arellano, 36; and Amalia Loyola, 48. In a TV interview shown all over the US, an anguished Nelia Arellano blamed the limo driver for failing to stop immediately and for cowardly refusing to help them get out of the burning limo.

http://www.washingtonpost.com/national/limo-passenger-to-driver-after-fire-help-me/2013/05/07/d4dfd631-e67b-4b16-b01b-503c68b0e28f_video.html?tid=obnetwork

As the TV camera started rolling, Ann posed the question to me:

"So why are there so many Filipino nurses in the US?"

I told her that Americans should not to be too surprised at the large number of Filipinos in the US. After all, the Philippines was a US colony from 1899 until the Japanese occupation in 1942 and, some would argue, a "neo-colony" for many decades after the Philippines was granted independence by the US in 1946. Just as it does not surprise the British to see many Indians and Pakistanis in England, nor does it surprise the French that there are many Algerians in France. They understand that people from the colonized countries generally tend to gravitate and immigrate to their "mother" countries, even long after their native countries were granted independence.

There are four waves of Filipino nurse immigration to the US. Actually, for the TV interview, I told Ann there were three.

FIRST WAVE

The first wave came after the US began its colonization of the Philippines and needed local health care professionals to meet the health needs of the subject population which is why the US Army recruited Filipinos to work as Volunteer Auxiliary and Contract Nurses.

Under the Pensionado Act of 1903, Filipinos were sent to the US as government-funded scholars (*pensionados*) including those pursuing a nurse education. Some of those who stayed for employment as nurses in the US went on to form the Philippine Nurses Association of New York in 1928. The association's first president was Marta Ubana, who completed her Bachelor of Science in Nursing degree at Teachers College, Columbia University.

Many other *pensionado* nurses returned back to the Philippines to help set up and manage the 17 nursing schools that were established in the Philippines from 1903 until 1940. Large numbers of the graduates from these nursing schools thereafter immigrated to the US as, unlike with the Chinese and Japanese, there were no immigration restrictions against them since Filipinos were considered "US nationals" and even traveled with US passports.

My friend, Lissa Sobrepena, came to my office two months ago and excitedly told me that she just learned that her grandmother, who died before she was born, had lived and worked in the US as an RN. She showed me the photos of her grandmother, Isabel Mina, which she saw by logging on to Ancestry.com. On it, she viewed various documents of her grandmother including the two passport applications of Isabel Mina who lost her US passport while traveling in the US.

Lissa learned that her grandmother had immigrated to the US in 1921 with two other Filipino nurses, Josefa Cariaga and Petra Aguinaldo, and that they all worked as RNs in Hawaii and California before moving on to New York.

Lissa then learned to her astonishment that her grandmother's best friend, Petra Aguinaldo, was the grandmother of her husband, Robert Sobrepena. Neither Lissa nor Robert knew that their grandmothers were nurses and were friends and that they had traveled together across the US.

SECOND WAVE

According to Catherine Ceniza Choy, associate professor of ethnic studies at the University of California, Berkeley, and author of *Empire of Care: Nursing and Migration in Filipino American History* (Duke University Press, 2003), the next big wave of nurses from the Philippines came began in1948, as part of the Exchange Visitor Program that was set up by the US State Department to "combat Soviet propaganda". Because of the "special relationship" between the mother country and its former colony, a large percentage of the exchange visitors came from the Philippines, and many of them were nurses.

Among these nurses was Maria Guerrero Llapitan who came to the US in 1948 to take post-graduate nursing courses at Baylor University in Texas. Maria had served as the supervisor of the operating room of a hospital in Bataan before it fell to the Japanese invaders in 1942.

After completing her postgraduate studies at Baylor, Maria moved to Chicago to work at the Cook County General Hospital where she met her fiance. She then went to Hunter College for Women in New York to get her nursing degree while working at Sloane-Kettering Memorial Hospital in New York.

Maria later married her fiancé in San Francisco where they set up a family in 1951. She later was among the Filipino nurses who formed the Philippine Nurses Association of Northern California in 1961.

THIRD WAVE

The third wave of Filipino nurse immigration to the US came after 1965 when US Immigration laws were liberalized to allow Filipino nurses and other professionals to immigrate to the US. It also allowed Filipino nurses to come to the US on tourist visas without prearranged employment and to then adjust their status in the US.

During this period, the number of nursing schools in the Philippines soared from 17 in 1940 to 170 in 1990 to more than 429 at the present time.

But only 15-20% of the Filipino nurses who immigrated to the US after 1965 could pass the state nursing board exams. This led to the establishment in 1977 of the Commission on Graduates of Foreign Nursing Schools (CGFNS) to help prevent the exploitation of graduates of foreign nursing schools who come to the United States to work as nurses but who can't pass the nursing board exams here.

The CGFNS developed a pre-immigration certification program that consisted of: a credentials review; a test of nursing knowledge (CGFNS qualifying examination), and an English-language proficiency examination (TOEFL).

Since 1977, CGFNS has administered more than 350,000 tests to approximately 185,000 applicants in 43 test sites worldwide. From 1978 to 2000, the data showed that 73% of CGFNS test takers came from the Philippines, followed by the United Kingdom (4%), India (3%), Nigeria (3%), and Ireland (3%).

ROLE MODEL

Menchu Sanchez immigrated to the US in 1980s and has worked as an RN for more than 25 years, the last three years at the New York University Langone Medical Center. When Superstorm Sandy battered New York last October, Menchu was taking care of 20 at-risk infants in the Intensive Care Unit of her hospital. Sandy knocked out the electric power to the hospital causing Menchu to organize the nurses and doctors to carry the babies in warming pads down 8 flights of stairs to safety. Menchu was invited to sit beside First Lady Michelle Obama at the State of the Nation Address (SONA) of Pres. Obama on February 12, 2013.

In his SONA speech, Pres. Obama cited Menchu as a role model: "We should follow the example of a New York City nurse named Menchu Sanchez. When Hurricane Sandy plunged her hospital into darkness, she wasn't thinking about how her own home was faring. Her mind was on the 20 precious newborns in her care and the rescue plan she devised that kept them all safe."

Many Filipino nurses who entered the US on H-1work visas after passing the CGFNS tests benefited from the passage of the Nursing Relief Act of 1989 which provided for their adjustment to permanent resident status if they had H-1 nonimmigrant status as registered nurses and had been employed in that capacity for at least 3 years.

But the "sunsetting" of this law in 1995 effectively decreased Filipino nurse immigration to the United States. The passage of the Illegal Immigration Reform and Immigrant Responsibility Act of 1998 (IIRIIRA) further discouraged nurse immigration to the US.

GROW YOUR OWN

The passage of restrictive legislation was fueled by xenophobic fears of foreign nurses as was expressed in July of 2009, when former Washington DC Mayor Marion Barry complained to the press: "In fact, it's so bad, that if you go to the hospital now, you find a number of immigrants who are nurses, particularly from the Philippines," Barry told the *Examiner*. "And no offense, but let's grow our own teachers, let's grow our own nurses -- and so that we don't have to be scrounging around in our community clinics and other kinds of places -- having to hire people from somewhere else."

Grow your own nurses the US did. According to the National Council of State Boards of Nursing, US nursing schools produced close to a million nurses from 2006 to 2011.

While the demand for Filipino nurses may have waned in the US, the demand for Filipino nurses in the rest of the world did not diminish. Filipino nurses working for the National Health System (NHS) in England drew national attention last February when Britain's 91-year-old Prince Philip, while on a tour of a new cardiac centre in Bedfordshire, England, turned to a Filipino nurse and said: "The Philippines must be half-empty – you're all here running the NHS."

Not quite, not by a long shot, your majesty.

According to Reuben Seguritan, general counsel of the Philippine Nurses Association of America (PNAA), the Philippines is the world's largest supplier of foreign-trained nurses with 429 nursing schools and 80,000 nursing students. To place this number in perspective, City College of San Francisco, with 89,000 students, does not have the resources to accept more than 75 students into its nursing program. The nursing students are chosen by lottery from a list of about 500 students who otherwise qualify for acceptance.

FOURTH WAVE

Is there a fourth wave of Filipino nurse immigration to the US?

Yes, but it hasn't arrived yet. According to recent CNN report, "Demand for health care services is expected to climb as more baby boomers retire and health care reform makes medical care accessible to more people. As older nurses start retiring, economists predict a massive nursing shortage will reemerge in the United States."

The CNN report adds: "We've been really worried about the future workforce because we've got almost 900,000 nurses over the age of 50 who will probably retire this decade, and we'll have to replace them," [economist and nurse Peter] Buerhaus said."

The fourth wave may come as early as 2014 when the US Patient Protection and Affordable Care Act, otherwise known as Obamacare, comes into effect and about 30-40 million Americans without any health insurance will finally be covered by health care insurance.

LPG Marketer's Association party-list Rep. Arnel Ty believes that Obamacare will "stimulate" the US hiring of foreign nurses. "This will hopefully spur a bit US demand for new foreign nurses and other health practitioners such as pharmacists, physical therapists, medical technologists, radiologists, and speech pathologists," Ty said.

As we reflect on the past and contemplate the future, let's all say a prayer for the repose of the souls of the five Filipino nurses who died in that limo fire on May 4 and pray also for the recovery of those nurses who were injured in that accident.

ooooo

19
Telltale Signs:
Philippines - a Jewish Refugee from the Holocaust

Dateline, 2013

The 1993 Oscar award for Best Picture, *Schindler's List,* informed the world about Austrian industrialist Oskar Schindler and how he saved 1,100 Polish Jews during WWII by hiring them as workers in his factory. A new documentary, *"Rescue in the Philippines: Refuge From the Holocaust,* being shown this month in hundreds of PBS stations throughout the US, will now inform the world about Philippine Commonwealth Pres. Manuel L. Quezon and the role he and others played in helping German Jews escape Nazi persecution in 1939 by providing them with visas and safe shelter in the Philippines.

http://rescueinthephilippines.com
The significance of Quezon's actions can best be understood in the context provided by another Hollywood movie, the 1976 film, *Voyage of the Damned,* based on the true story of the 1939 saga of the luxury liner MS *St.Louis*, which left Hamburg, Germany with 937 Jewish passengers bound for Cuba. When the ship landed in Havana, the Jews were refused entry,

as the Nazi authorities expected. The ship then headed for Florida where the US government also refused to allow the Jews to disembark. After the ship was refused entry in other ports, it returned to Germany where its Jewish passengers were forcibly removed and dispatched to concentration camps for extermination. A Nazi official in the film declares: *"When the whole world has refused to accept them as refugees, no country can blame Germany for the fate of the Jews."*

But at least one country can. In the year when the MS St. Louis was rejected by all the countries where it sought refuge, the Philippine Commonwealth accepted 1,300 Jews and was willing to accept as much as 10,000 more if the US State Department had allowed its commonwealth to do so.

The *Washington Times* reported on December 5, 1938 (*"Quezon Urges Jews' Haven"*) that "the possibility of a haven for Jewish refugees from Germany was broached today by Pres. Manuel Quezon" who said "I am willing to facilitate entrance of such numbers of Jewish people as we could absorb…I favor large scale immigration to Mindanao, if well financed.

The untold story of the Philippine rescue of Jews was first prominently recounted by Frank Ephraim in his book, *"Escape to Manila: From Nazi Tyranny to Japanese Terror"* (University of Illinois Press, 2003), which was based mostly on his own eyewitness account as a child who was one of 1300 Jewish refugees who arrived in Manila in 1939.

According to Ephraim, the history of the rescue began with the decision of the Frieder brothers in 1918 to relocate its two-for-a-nickel cigar business from Manhattan to Manila, where production would be cheaper. Alex, Philip, Herbert and Morris Frieder took turns overseeing the business in the Philippines for two years each joining a community that had fewer than 200 Jews. At its height, the Frieder brothers' tobacco company in Manila produced 250 million cigars in a year.

The idea for the Jewish exodus to the Philippines likely came in 1937, when 28 German Jews who had earlier fled Germany for Shanghai were evacuated by the Germans to Manila after fierce fighting erupted between Chinese and Japanese troops. The Jewish Refugee Committee in Manila, headed by Philip Frieder, was formed to help them settle in the Philippines. From these refugees, the Frieders heard first-hand accounts of the Nazi atrocities in Germany and the uncertain fate of the 17,000 Jews still stranded in Shanghai.

The Frieders decided to seek the help of their poker buddies to get the Philippines to become a haven for the fleeing Jews. But these were no ordinary poker buddies. One was Paul V. McNutt, the American High Commissioner for the Philippines; another was a young officer named Col. Dwight D. Eisenhower, the aide of Gen. Douglas MacArthur, then Field Marshall of the Philippines; and then there was Manuel L. Quezon, the president of the Philippine Commonwealth.

In their late night poker sessions, as Ephraim recounts it, the buddies hatched a plan for the Philippines to accept as many as 100,000 Jews to save them from persecution in Germany.

McNutt had served as National Commander of the American Legion and as governor of Indiana (1933-37) before Pres. Franklin D. Roosevelt tapped him to be the High Commissioner of the Philippines in 1937. McNutt's task was to convince the US State Department to grant visas for Jews to enter Manila.

Col. Eisenhower's task was to organize a plan to bring Jews to settle in Mindanao. In the *Rescue in the Philippines* documentary,Susan Eisenhower, President Dwight Eisenhower's granddaughter, reflects on his involvement: "I think for my grandfather, it was perhaps that simple. You have a country. You have a little authority. You have an opportunity. Someone has asked for refuge—which is the most basic humanitarian appeal anyone can make. You answer it."

Pres. Quezon faced the formidable task of winning over the anti-Semitic members of his own cabinet as well as those in the political opposition led by Gen. Emilio Aguinaldo who viewed Jews as "Communists and schemers" bent on "controlling the world". In a letter written in August of 1939, Alex Frieder wrote of Mr. Quezon's response: "*He assured us that big or little, he raised hell with every one of those persons. He made them ashamed of themselves for being a victim of propaganda intended to further victimize an already persecuted people.*"

To the members of his own Catholic Church who were prejudiced against Jews, Quezon asked: "How can we turn our backs on the race that produced Jesus Christ?"

At the April 23, 1940 dedication of Marikina Hall, a housing facility for Jewish refugees that was built on land that he personally donated, Quezon said: "*It is my hope and, indeed, my expectation that the people of the Philippines will have in the future every reason to be glad that when the time of need came, their country was willing to extend a hand of welcome.*"

Quezon's expectation of how future generations of Filipinos will feel about the rescue of the Jews during their time of peril had one flaw: the future generations never learned of the country's noble deed. After the *Rescue* documentary was shown at its April 7, 2013 San Francisco premiere, a question and answer forum followed. One Filipina from Vallejo stood up and identified herself as having been a public school teacher in the Philippines before immigrating to the US. "How is it possible that I never heard of this Jewish rescue when I was a student in the Philippines, when I was a teacher there, all the way until I watched this film tonight?" she asked.

The answers provided by other Filipinos in the audience ("*because it was not taught in Philippine history books*") begged the question of why this significant event in Philippine history was omitted from the Philippine history books.

I went to elementary school at Letran College in Intramuros, Manila. Every day, for the 8 years I was there from kindergarten to

7th grade, I passed by the imposing bronze statue of Manuel L. Quezon, the school's most distinguished alumnus. I thought I knew everything there was to know about Quezon until I stumbled on Frank Ephraim's book in 2005 and learned for the first time about Quezon's role as a "righteous gentile" and wrote about it then.

http://www.beyondchron.org/news/index.php?itemid=2620

Why was this heroic act hidden from the Filipino people? Why was it not included in Philippine history books? Strangely enough, what is recounted in the history books is that on November 29,1947, the Philippines was the only Asian nation to support the partition resolution at the United Nations creating a Jewish State in Palestine.

On June 21, 2009, a monument to Manuel L. Quezon was unveiled at the 65-hectare Holocaust Memorial Park in Rishon LeZion, Israel's 4th largest city located south of Tel Aviv. The monument designed by Filipino artist Junyee is called "Open Doors". It is a geometric, seven-meter-high sculpture rendered mainly in steel and set on a base of marble tiles shipped from Romblon, showing three doors of ascending heights.

Speaking at the dedication ceremonies on behalf of the Philippine government, Tourism Secretary Joseph Durano said: "the monument celebrates the Filipino heart, a heart that touches others with compassion, a heart that makes one a blessing to the world."

But that Filipino heart desperately needs to know about the noble act that made it a blessing to the world.

Ooooo

20
Telltale Signs: OFW Remittances Promote Mendicant Culture
Dateline, 2013

A Philippine cabinet-level agency official announced on September 10 that for the last 3 years, the country has become "less dependent" on remittances from Overseas Filipino Workers (OFW) but admitted that the country cannot hope to achieve "zero dependence" from OFW remittances due to its "important role in promoting inclusive growth or economic growth that trickles down to the masses (which) are used to address various household needs such as food, shelter, and education."

Planning Director Rosemarie Edillon of the National Economic Development Authority (NEDA) added that apart from the "trickle down" benefits of remittances, "our country's international reserves have been at comfortable levels, and this implies less vulnerability of the country to external shocks, lesser reliance on foreign savings, and availability of more currency that will help our country service its debts and pay its imports. "

The cash remittances by Filipinos working and living overseas, according to the *Bangko Sentral ng Pilipinas* (BSP), reached $1.809 billion in July, growing 5.4% year-on-year, hitting $11.94 billion for seven months in 2012 so far, "higher by 5.2% from $11.35 billion the previous year."

At least one million Filipinos leave the Philippines every year to work abroad, reaching a current total estimated at between 9.5 million to 12.5 million Filipinos working overseas, according to the figures of the Overseas Workers Welfare Administration (OWWA).

This massive migration of Filipinos to more than 210 countries around the world was the subject of a short documentary recently shown on America's Current TV network

(www.youtube.com/watch?v=N7rVibDs WKo&feature=fvst) which opened with this line: "Imagine a nation where the #1 career choice is leaving the country."

Although the country is "rich in culture and resources", the introduction adds, much of the population wants to leave. Where? *Destination, Anywhere*" is the answer and the title of the documentary.

One *Foreign Policy Blog* article describes the documentary as focusing on the impact of remittances on the Philippines. But the interviews of OFWs in the documentary show them merely explaining why they are sending money back to their families in the Philippines - "to feed my family", "to pay for family medical expenses" were the most common reasons offered.

One segment in the film shows a crowded Metro Manila mall where a local bank advertises that customers can receive their remittances there. The Current reporter comments that it is a most convenient location because remittance recipients can then spend their parents' hard-earned dollars on the luxury items that abound in the mall.

Gloria Navarrete, a long-time South San Francisco resident, related how she sought to provide income opportunities to the young people in her hometown of Lipa City, Batangas. "I offered to pay the kids good money to pick the *lanzones* fruits in my brother's farm so they can be sold in the market," she said. "But they refused to do any work because they didn't need the money, they said. Their relatives abroad were sending them money regularly so they didn't have to work if they didn't want to."

"I know one family of 4 kids who were receiving money regularly from their mother who works 24/7 as a domestic helper in Long Island, New York," she said. "The kids refused to do any work because they have enough money for their cell phone bills and food and miscellaneous living expenses."

There is a term to describe the kids who rely on remittances, and not their own hard-earned labor, for their daily living expenses. They are "mendicants" and the society that is bred by this "new form of social illness" is the subject of a new documentary by Ted Unarce entitled "**Mendicant Society**" which will hold its world premiere at the Third World Independent Film Festival

(*thirdworldindiefilmfest.com*) this Friday, September 21, at 4:30 PM at the Century 20 Theatre at the Great Mall Plaza in Milpitas, California.

Catch the trailer on Youtube: http://www.youtube.com/watch?v=FA FLEc8_rp0.

"Many of us ponder the factors behind the creation of corruption in our youth, our culture, our politicians, even our families," Unarce explains in his synopsis of his film. "By taking a look at the issue broadly, we might ask how an entire society can lose its balance due to lack of morals, principles, discipline, hope, and other factors."

Mendicant Society examines the Philippines as a case in point, Unarce explains, because of its "long history of government-sponsored human exportation which adds a great sense of calculated malignancy to this problem by creating a society that sustains itself by way of remittances from family members working abroad and by supporting a national government that lends itself to being mendicant to the very people it serves."

The narrative in the documentary could have been provided by Gloria Navarrete because it mirrors her own frustrating experience with the young people of her hometown. "Given the scarcity of employment opportunities in the Philippines, family members left behind often begin to self-identify as hopeless and helpless victims of circumstance. To compound this dilemma, these family members receive remittances, at-first an enticing prospect which gives them very little motivation to seek employment themselves. The figurative door is thrown open to sloth, greed and corruption."

There is an intriguing quote from Jewish-American writer Anzia Yezierska at the start of the *Mendicant Society* documentary - "Give a beggar a dime and he'll bless you. Give him a dollar and he'll curse you for withholding the rest of your fortune. Poverty is a bag with a hole in the bottom."

The "dollar" perhaps represents the significant remittances sent by hard-working parents to their children in the Philippines who somehow believe they are entitled to the money and to the rest of the "fortune" provided by their parents. The remittances are soon wasted away on frivolous items, like a bag with a hole in the bottom perpetuating the cycle of poverty. The remittances are not a blessing but a curse.

Philippine government bureaucrats present the upside of the issue - remittances are necessary for national development because they provide funds for food, shelter and education for millions of Filipinos dependent on them for their daily sustenance. And, by the way, they provide economic stability to the Philippine economy and government.

Mendicant Society provides the downside.

Ooooo

21

422 Years Ago

Dateline: INQUIRER.net
First Posted October 15, 2009
Filed Under: CALIFORNIA, United States –

Historical records do not cite the names of any of the "Luzon Indios" aboard the Nuestra Senora de Buena Esperanza when it landed in Morro Bay, California on October 18, 1587.

All we know of the people who would later be called "Filipinos" was that the Esperanza's captain, Pedro De Unamuno, wrote in his log that his crew was composed of "Luzon Indios." All the natives of the Spanish colonies were called "Indios."

According to Unamuno's account, because his ship needed to replenish its supplies after two months at sea, he had to dock in the nearest land even if it was not found on any of the Spanish maps, a land that would later be called California.

Unamuno wrote that he sent two groups to explore the land, one group of 12 soldiers which he personally led, and a group of Luzon Indios led by a Franciscan priest, Fr. Martin Ignacio De Loyola. Fr. Loyola carried a cross while his Indios were armed with swords and shields.

While reconnoitering the new land, the Luzon Indios encountered a group of five males, two females, and two babies that may similarly be called California Indios. But the natives ran from them to avoid any contact. Father De Loyola and his Indios then returned back to the Esperanza.

The following day, October 19, Unamuno ventured on shore again with 12 Spanish soldiers and eight Luzon Indios led this time by Fr. Francisco De Noguera. Two of the indios were sent ahead to scout the terrain. They found a camp with 17 dugouts of varying sizes that had just been abandoned by the natives who were eager to avoid contact. After failing to make contact with any of the natives, Unamuno and his crew then camped out.

While Unamuno and his crew were exploring the land, Fr. Martin and another crew of Luzon Indios went ashore to get wood and fresh water for the ship and to wash their clothes at a nearby creek. As they were doing so, a group of 23 natives approached them to ask them what they were doing. As there was a language problem, they could not understand each other. Because of their superior numbers, the natives were able to seize the clothes the Luzon Indios were washing and their water canteens. When they tried to seize Fr. Martin, gun shots came from the ship, forcing the natives to withdraw.

On Tuesday, October 20, Unamuno and his soldiers were nearing their ship when they saw two Luzon Indios running down from a hill, under attack from the natives. Unamuno's soldiers went up the hill to repulse the attackers. Three of his soldiers were wounded including one fatally. Unamuno reported that a Luzon Indio was also killed by "a javelin which he failed to ward off with his shield."

After a prolonged battle, Unamuno and his crew returned to the Esperanza and decided to continue their voyage to Acapulco on October 21 reaching Acapulco on November 22, 1587.

It would take another eight years before another group of Filipinos would return to California.

On November 6, 1595, a Spanish galleon ship, the San Agustin, landed in what is now Point Reyes in Marin County in the San Francisco Bay Area. The Spaniards christened the bay "La Bahia de San Francisco" but it would take another century for the bay across from Point Reyes to be called that name.

In his San Francisco Chronicle article (400th Anniversary Of Spanish Shipwreck, November 14, 1995), Carl Nolte wrote "the San Agustin, which was probably a small warship in the Spanish navy, was commanded by Sebastian Rodriguez Cermeno and had a crew of Spanish officers and Filipino sailors, according to historian Raymond Aker, who has studied the ship and its voyage. The expedition turned out badly: The San Agustin was the first ship known to be wrecked on the California coast."

The San Agustin's voyage began in the summer of 1595 when it sailed from Manila to Acapulco with a cargo of 130 tons of Ming Dynasty porcelain, silk, and other trade goods from China bound for Spain. It was part of the Manila-Acapulco Galleon Trade that would dominate the economy of the Philippine colony from 1565 to 1815.

On occasion, a galleon ship would also carry gold and silver, extracted from Philippine mines. This was the case with the Santa Ana, a galleon ship that left Manila the year after Pedro

De Unamuno's voyage, in 1588. It was hijacked by English pirates off the coast of Mexico.

When the San Agustin landed in Point Reyes, the ship's Spanish officers wanted to quickly resume the voyage to Acapulco but Captain Cermeno wanted to explore the land. By then the ship had made contact with the local natives, the Coast Miwoks, who lived in about six villages in the area. Cermeno gave them cloths and other gifts while the Miwoks gave them seeds and a banner of black feathers.

At Cermeno's direction, the Filipino sailors "assembled a small launch on the beach for exploring the shallow waters nearby. They stayed at the bay for three weeks, in gentle fall weather." Unfortunately, a storm came which pulled the ship's anchor up and blew the ship to the rocks, killing a dozen men including a priest.

What happened to the cargo of the San Agustin? According to Nolte, "The Miwoks picked up the cargo, slept on the silk meant for the royalty of Europe, ate from the priceless blue porcelain of the Wan Li period of the Ming Dynasty."

Captain Cermeno and his crew of Filipino sailors and a dog then built a larger launch from the materials they could find in Point Reyes and sailed out to Acapulco, which they reached without losing a man. They did lose the dog, though, which the Filipino crew and their Spanish captain ate to survive.

ooooo

22
Filipino American History Month

Dateline, INQUIRER.net
First Posted November 5, 2009
Filed Under: CALIFORNIA

If you google "Chinese American History Month" or "Japanese American History Month," the search engine will direct you to "Asian Pacific American Heritage Month," enacted into law on October 28, 1992 to honor the achievements of Asian/Pacific Americans and their contributions to the US.

All 30 or so Asian ethnic groups in the US were lumped together as "Asian Pacific Americans" and given one month (May) to celebrate their collective and individual cultures, histories, and heritage in the United States. The month of May was chosen because the first Japanese immigrants arrived in the United States on May 7, 1843 and the transcontinental railroad, which employed hundreds of Chinese immigrant laborers, was completed on May 10, 1869 (Golden Spike Day).

It actually started out as "Asian Pacific American Heritage Week" when President Jimmy Carter signed the Joint Resolution on October 2, 1978 but it became a month-long celebration in 1992 when President George H.W. Bush signed the law permanently designating May of each year as Asian Pacific American Heritage Month.

But Filipino Americans were never satisfied with being lumped together with other "Asian Pacific Americans" in celebrating May because for one, May's only significant event for Filipinos was when the US Navy destroyed the Spanish armada in Manila Bay on May 1, 1898, which victory paved the way for the US colonization of the Philippines.

As a publicly elected official in San Francisco for 18 years, I regularly attended the annual kick-off celebration of Asian Pacific American Heritage Month in San Francisco's City Hall. It would always be awkward for me when Japanese Americans would recount the day in May of 1843 when the first Japanese arrived in the US and Chinese Americans would celebrate the day in May of 1869 when the Chinese-built transcontinental railroad was completed and I could not celebrate that day in May of 1898 when Dewey destroyed the Spanish Fleet which later resulted in the US suppression of our Philippine independence. ("Hurray, we've been invaded and colonized!")

For years since its founding in Seattle, Washington in 1982, it was always the goal of the Filipino American National History Society (FANHS) for Filipino Americans to be given our very own month to celebrate our history and culture in the United States.

At its biennial national conference in 1988, FANHS members unanimously passed a resolution "to establish Filipino American History Month to be observed annually and nationally throughout the United States and its Territories during the Month of October commencing in the Year 1992 to mark the 405th Anniversary of the Presence of Filipinos in the Continental United States."

The resolution also believed that such a month-long celebration would be "a significant time to study the advancement of Filipino Americans in the history of the United States, as a favorable time of celebration, remembrance, reflection, and motivation, and as a relevant time to renew more efforts toward research, examination, and promulgation of Filipino American history and culture in order to provide an opportunity for all Americans to learn and appreciate more about Filipino Americans and their historic contributions to our nation, these United States of America."

Just as Japanese Americans could celebrate the day the first Japanese immigrants landed in California in May of 1843, Filipino Americans could now also proudly commemorate the day the first Filipinos ("Luzon Indios") landed in California on October 18, 1587, more than 33 years before the first English immigrants landed on Plymouth Rock in 1620.

Beginning in 1989, Filipino Americans began celebrating October as Filipino American History Month with celebrations and festivities throughout the US. Various states, aside from California and Hawaii, would routinely pass resolutions as Michigan Governor Jennifer Granhom did when she proclaimed "October 2006, as Filipino American Heritage Month in Michigan, and I encourage all citizens to recognize, applaud, and participate in this celebration of the many contributions made by Filipino Americans that enhance the quality of life in Michigan."

But the celebration in various states somehow just wasn't enough. As the Wikipedia entry on this subject noted, "October as Filipino American History Month has not yet attained the prestige of other similar minority celebrations, such as the Black History Month in February, Women's History Month in March, and the Asian Pacific American Heritage Month in May. This is evidenced by the fact that no United States Congress has ever resolved to recognize Filipino American History Month."

That Wikipedia entry now needs to be updated. On November 3, 2009, Representative Stephen Lynch (D-Massachusetts) stood up on the House floor to announce that on October 29, 2009, the House Oversight and Government Reform Committee had unanimously approved House Resolution 780 celebrating October as Filipino American History Month. It was originally sponsored by Rep. Bob Filner (D-California) with over 50 members of the House signing on as co-sponsors. Rep. Lynch also announced that the US Senate had unanimously passed a similarly worded resolution (S. 298) on October 1, 2009. He asked for the unanimous consent of the House to make the bill into law.

Before the vote could take place, Rep. Patrick McHenry (R- North Carolina) stood up and deplored the lack of substantive resolutions being passed by the House but joined Rep. Lynch in asking for the unanimous consent of the House for HR 780.

When the call was made for the vote, it was passed unanimously. October is now Filipino American History Month in the United States!

Ooooo

23
Why I Publish/Reprint Books
Tatay Jobo Blizes
Self-Publisher

Writings are timeless and they act as mirrors to history. I publish writings as they remain relevant anytime. I have seen a lot of good writings in the internet, in magazines and newspapers. But most writers have only one or two articles and therefore not enough material to be published as a book. And yet, many of them need to be published or archived. There are also writers who write a lot but never publish them. There are also old books with no more prints available. The solution is to publish/reprint.

I do this for free because of the print-books-on-demand (POD) system, but the printed or hardcopy is not free

The printed book will always be there among your collections or libraries. Not all use the internet. The internet access has its technical problems. I can produce fiction, non-fiction, in color also.

My booklist can be seen at http://tinyurl.com/mj76ccq (copy and paste)

Permission had been granted by the author/ authors to print their books under my free self-publishing service. They own copyrights to their works.

Interested reader may request free reading of any of my books, articles or essays via online reading or ebook. Just email me. Thank you.

ooooo